REST
OLD

MICHÈLE BROWN

Michèle Brown was born in Swansea and took a degree in Modern History at St Anne's College, Oxford. She then worked as a television and radio reporter and presenter, giving many talks about restoring furniture on programmes such as *Woman's Hour* and Thames Television's *Good Afternoon*. She has also written a regular column on the subject for *Living* magazine.

Her other books include *Restoration and Repair*, *Queen Elizabeth II – the Silver Jubilee Book*, the *Little Royal Book*, *Food by Appointment*, the *Royal Year Book*, and two children's books – *Fun to Know about Dogs* and *Fun to Know about Dinosaurs*.

Michèle now lives in London and has the full-time job of looking after her three young children. However, she still finds time for her favourite hobby – restoring old junk!

RESTORING OLD JUNK

Michèle Brown

**Illustrated with line drawings
by David Farris**

Hamlyn Paperbacks

RESTORING OLD JUNK

ISBN 0 600 37635 4

First published
in Great Britain 1973 by
Lutterworth Press
Hamlyn Paperbacks edition 1979
Copyright © Michèle Brown 1973

Hamlyn Paperbacks are published by
The Hamlyn Publishing Group Ltd.,
Astronaut House,
Feltham,
Middlesex, England

Set, printed and bound in Great Britain by
Cox & Wyman Ltd.,
London, Reading and Fakenham

For
MY MOTHER

RESTORING
OLD JUNK

Contents

Introduction

This is a book for people who have a real enthusiasm for old things but who, like me, find the present-day prices of antiques almost unbelievably high.

The methods I describe will cope with almost any piece of junk you want to restore, but I've avoided those which require the sort of equipment you'd only expect to find on an expensively equipped, professional work bench. However, there are some cheap tools and bits of equipment you will find it difficult to do without: a piece of old lino, or something similar, to protect your working surface; rubber gloves and disposable surgical gloves; Araldite; paint stripper, with which you can also clean your brushes; a small cabriole head hammer which combines a nail extractor with a hammer head; a hand drill with assorted bits; a small screwdriver; a jar of assorted nails and screws; paint brushes; turpentine substitute (white spirit); a cupboard with a lock and key, so that you can keep tools, equipment, etc., safe from children – almost anything, even a nail, can cause trouble in a child's hands.

The hardware department in a store like Woolworth's stocks practically all the straightforward things you will need, plus a few others you've never even thought of, like a profile gauge (which is very useful for copying any shapes you want to cut round) and a rack for keeping your tools tidy.

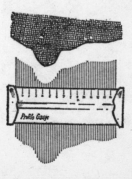

The yellow pages in the telephone directory are invaluable for looking up places which provide useful services such as making loose covers or selling upholstery materials.

It's a good idea to be realistic about what you really *will* get around to doing and avoid lumbering yourself with true junk, which just hangs about making you feel guilty until you finally decide to throw it out.

It is also a good idea to be able to sum up the possibilities of a piece of junk quickly – especially at an auction. This is a skill you soon acquire after restoring one or two items, especially if you have a good knowledge of what you are aiming for or trying to copy. It helps to browse round the museums and to read lots of books about antique and Victorian furniture and decoration. You will also then be better able to decide if your new acquisition needs professional attention. If it does, the British Antiques Yearbook has a list of reputable restorers, and it's a book available in any public library.

It pays to get to know the people at the local Do-It-Yourself shop, where you can get a lot of good advice free and find out about any new time- or effort-saving products available. There is no great virtue in doing something in a tedious, old-fashioned way if it can be avoided. After all, restoring junk shouldn't be an exhausting chore; with just a bit of practice it can be an interesting and profitable pastime.

China

Introduction

Old china is just about the cheapest type of junk you can buy. Yet many of the old dinner and tea services were extremely beautiful. Often one isolated piece survives from a high quality service, made by a factory like Wedgwood or Royal Doulton. Like gold and silver, good china can be identified by the maker's mark. There are far too many of these for most people to be familiar with them all, but if you are interested you can buy a small booklet on the subject and carry it with you (details are given in the book list on page 114).

Auction sales are probably the best places to buy old china cheaply as the dealers are usually more interested in the larger items. For very little expense you can build up a 'Harlequin' set of coffee cups or dinner plates from incomplete sets of really good quality china. Many dinner plates are hand-painted and look attractive as wall decorations. You can either buy ready-made supports for these in hardware shops or improvise them yourself from wire.

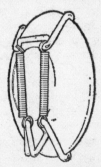

Old china wash sets of jug and basin can be bleached and sterilised with sodium hypochlorite (Milton) according to the maker's instructions to turn them into useful table china– the basin makes a marvellous salad bowl when you have a lot of people to feed. Soup tureens are often left over when the rest of a dinner service is broken and the shape makes them ideal for use as a rose bowl, by simply putting some crumpled-up chicken wire in the base.

Since china is so fragile, don't be too disappointed if your efforts at repair end in disaster – after all, it's only junk. Like everything else, mending china takes practice. By tackling the easier cases first you'll acquire skill and an intuition for what you can and can't do.

Cleaning

Some junk china may need no more than a good clean to make it usable again. A shiny glaze is almost always painted on to a finished piece of china before it is fired. This may develop hairline cracks (probably through being overheated) in which the dirt of many years accumulates, emphasising the cracks and making the piece look far more disreputable than it really is. Usually these hairline cracks seem to 'disappear' completely when cleaned.

Washing

Washing the piece in warm water and a good washing-up liquid may be sufficient. If it is made of metal or wood as well as china, don't immerse it in water but wipe the china parts with a cloth wrung out in warm water and detergent, and 'rinse' them with a cloth wrung out in warm water alone.

The dirt may be rather stubborn so you may need to scrub gently along the cracks with an old toothbrush, using neat washing-up liquid. You can use a scouring pad – Brillo, for instance – in really bad cases, but take care not to scrub off any unglazed decoration.

Be careful not to make matters *worse* when cleaning china. If you immerse it in very hot water you may well cause more of the hairline cracks you are trying to disguise. It is worth testing a sample area first, where the damage is least likely to be seen, by wiping it over with a cloth wrung out in very hot water. If washing fails try 'Stainfree' tablets, available from chemists and hardware stores. These dissolve in hot water and make an effective solution which deals with most stains in about an hour. Try a second time if the first treatment doesn't seem sufficiently effective.

Bleaching

Bleaching may be necessary if the dirt is so firmly ingrained that the raw edges of the china are stained. This is more likely to be true of wide cracks but it can happen with the fine network of hairline cracks as well. For this purpose a mild bleach like sodium hypochlorite (Milton) or hydrogen peroxide is ideal. Always start cautiously and increase the strength of the bleach solution until it is adequate for the job. Begin by wiping it on to the crack with a wad of cotton wool. If this doesn't work, and it may well not be enough to remove old glue stains, then wring out a pad in the bleach solution and press it firmly on to the stained part. Leave the bleaching pad on and renew as often as necessary.

Removing grease

Methylated spirit applied with a clean cotton rag will remove grease on china as well as on wood and other materials.

Hygiene

If you are intending to eat off or drink from any of the old china you are restoring, you can ensure that pieces are germ-free by soaking them in Milton or in any of the similar preparations used for keeping babies' bottles sterile.

Mending

Riveting

Until recently china that was worth mending was usually riveted together, unless it was simply going to be placed in a display cabinet. Riveting is a tricky job, strictly for the experts. It is undoubtedly very strong, but it cannot be made really waterproof, and it is extremely ugly.

Dowelling

Dowelling is most often used when mending figures which have been broken in half or where some part of the figure, such as the head, has been knocked off, and the break is reasonably clean. It is done on exactly the same principle as dowelling wooden furniture, which is described on page 81. Two small holes are drilled, one into each surface, at a corresponding point. A small brass pin is cemented into one hole, with a glue such as Araldite. The other hole is then slipped over the pin and glued into place. Like riveting, this is really a professional job, but an amateur can often get quite good results with a small hand drill and strong nerves.

Adhesives

Modern adhesives are so greatly improved that sticking should be sufficient for all repairs. Certainly there is no need to resort to riveting for an article which is only intended for display. Epoxy adhesives, the standard or fast-drying types such as Araldite or Araldite Rapid, are best for mending china, especially if it will be in use. These adhesives are mixed from two components; all you have to do is to follow the maker's instructions. The idea is that the two surfaces you are joining together should be as smooth and flat as possible, and that there should be no air left in the join. There is no need to use a lot of adhesive to get a good result; in fact, being over-generous gives poor results. Although, unlike old-style glues, epoxy adhesives will not dissolve in water, you should still take care when washing any mended piece not to let the water get too hot.

It is possible to fill in chips and cracks, and there is some advice about this on pages 19–20, but usually it is best to give up really fragmented cases for lost, especially if any of the pieces are missing.

The two jobs which you are most likely to wish to tackle are SIMPLE FRACTURES, where the breaks are clean and none of the pieces is missing, and RE-ASSEMBLY – that is, either taking apart a piece of china which has been mended with rivets and mending it invisibly with glue, or, if it has already been glued and the old glue has discoloured, so that the join is obvious, doing the job again.

If the glue has discoloured, this usually indicates that it is one of the old-type glues, and it will dissolve if you put the article to soak in detergent and warm water. If this fails, a modern glue may have been used. Many manufacturers make solvents specifically for their own adhesives. An example is Evostick Cleaner which is intended for contact adhesives but which may work on other types and is worth trying when you do not know what adhesive has been used. New products like this are constantly coming on the market and it is worth an occasional browse around your Do-It-Yourself shop to keep up with developments. If proprietary adhesive solvents fail, acetone or methylated spirit may do the trick. Rivets can be filed through with a metal file, and carefully prised out, rather as if they were ordinary staples.

In all these cases the following method of re-sticking applies:

1. *Clean* the edges which are to be glued together. The cleaner they are, the firmer the join will be. Wipe them with methylated spirit to remove any grease.

2. *Bleach* stained edges using a mild bleach such as sodium hypochlorite (Milton), or the join will be clearly visible.

3. *Fit* the pieces together like a jigsaw puzzle before you start, to make sure they match. It saves time if you do this early on, as many pieces are almost identical and unless you assemble the whole pattern you could easily go astray. Epoxy adhesives are extremely difficult to remove once they have set, and they go tacky very quickly, so once the adhesive has been applied, you won't be able to spend time manoeuvring each piece into position.

4. *Work out* the order in which you will do the job, so that it is as simple as possible. Each case is different, of course, and you may well need to leave the partially mended article for a

day between stages, so that one glued-in piece is strong enough to support another.

5. *A warm atmosphere* makes the adhesive work better. It is worth warming the pieces you are going to stick together. A shelf above a radiator is a good place for actually doing the job.

6. *Follow the instructions* on the packet for mixing the two components of the epoxy adhesive. Apply the glue *thinly* to both sides of the break and press firmly together. Any surplus that oozes out should be carefully wiped away, if you can do this without risking pushing the two pieces out of position. Failing this, the surplus can be wiped away with solvent when the join is firm – be careful, though, not to let this solvent get into the newly-cemented join. But if surplus glue goes on to any *gilt* decoration, such as the rim of a hand-painted tea-cup, it *must* be wiped off immediately; if you leave it and try to wipe it off later with solvent, the gilt will come off too.

7. *Pressure* should be applied to keep the pieces together as tightly as possible. Usually this can be done by sticking gummed paper or Elastoplast at right angles *across* the join, as shown in the illustration. It is useless to stick paper or Elastoplast *along* the direction of the mend because it won't pull the two sides together. The advantage of using gummed strip, which you can buy in any stationer's, is that it has to be damped to make it stick: it will shrink as it dries and so will pull the two sides even closer together.

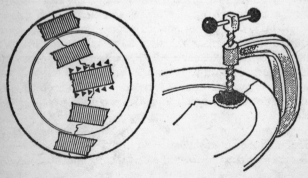

For more complex joins you can buy special clamps at Do-It-Yourself shops. Always put a small piece of felt between the china and the clamp.

Alternatively, you can improvise by using wedges or a box of sand – a glued-together bowl, for example, can be placed in a box and sand poured round it to hold the pieces in position while the adhesive dries.

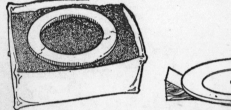

8. *Heating* in an oven will harden the joins further. To do this you should bake the article for not more than an hour, at a temperature of not more than 95°C (200°F) or, on a gas regulo, $\frac{1}{4}$. This is liable to cause cracking in the glaze if the temperature is not kept low; check frequently. It may also discolour the glue. A less drastic method is to place the mended article somewhere warm and dry, such as an airing cupboard or a shelf over a radiator.

Some cracks in china can be quite spectacular, and in such cases the intrepid repairer will usually complete the break and then glue the pieces back together. Occasionally it's sufficient simply to clean the crack. However, it's better, even without completing the break, to glue the crack together with epoxy adhesive, after cleaning, to prevent the dirt getting in again. Follow exactly the method already described for ordinary joins, prising the crack apart to insert the glue.

When you are more adept at sticking bits of china together, you can try colouring the adhesive to match the china, using powder pigments from art shops.

Filling Chips and Cracks
Adhesives coloured with art shop powder pigments can be

used as fillers for chips and wide cracks. To make a white filler, for instance, you mix titanium dioxide with your adhesive, and apply it with a small palette knife. Alternatively, if you do not feel like mixing your own filler, you can use a proprietary one like Barbola paste, again available from an art shop. This can be made up to any consistency, and for ordinary filling jobs is used like putty. Barbola paste is water soluble and should not be used on china which will come into contact with water.

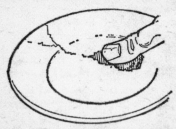

Whichever filler you use, slightly overfill the chip or crack to allow for shrinkage. You may get air bubbles if you try to slap it all in at once, so apply it carefully, a layer at a time, making sure it is firm and well packed down. Do allow a couple of days before getting to the fun job of re-painting or you may find the filler shrinks after painting and all your hard work falls away. Any excess filler can be scraped away with a razor blade, after the drying-out process has been completed, or rubbed down with wet and dry paper. Use a dry paper on Barbola paste.

Modelling Missing Pieces
For modelling missing pieces use Barbola paste mixed to the consistency of modelling clay. There is a great deal of fun to be had from this, and results depend really on how artistic you are. If a hand, for instance, is missing from a figure, you can try to copy freehand and stick the result on at the original break when it has dried. You can use a filler made with epoxy adhesive and titanium dioxide for modelling, but this is more difficult to work with because of its sticky consistency.

If you attempt to model a missing cup handle, strengthen it with a wire core.

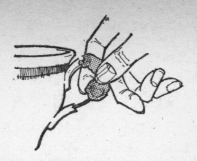

Painting and Glazing Mended China

Here again, results really depend on how artistic you are. Use fine brushes, available from art shops. If you want to match up a painted pattern, you can use artists' oils, which are useful as by mixing them you can get a wide range of colours.

If you have used a filler to fill in chips and cracks, or have modelled and stuck on substitute hands, flowers, etc., the mends and joins will still look different from the basic glazed china, since they are unglazed. A piece of glazed china which has been mended like this cannot be re-glazed to hide the repairs, but a good result can be achieved by painting the mended area with clear polyurethane varnish (or even colourless nail polish if you are in a hurry).

Instead of using oils and a varnish, you can try one of the proprietary products like Cryla or Darwi, which are sold in art shops. They come in a wide range of colours, including gold and silver, which are useful if you wish to reproduce gilding.

Dolls

Many old dolls were made from porcelain and the techniques for mending and decorating ordinary china apply equally well to them – in fact, dolls' faces give wonderful scope for anyone with artistic flair. The methods described in the last chapter of this book will then help you to tackle the clothes.

Glass

Introduction

Glass can be treated very much like china when you're cleaning and mending it.

Like china, most glass bargains are to be found in job lots at auctions, which are overlooked by the dealers. You may well come across simple acid-engraved decanters which are cheap because they were produced in fairly large numbers in the nineteenth century. Their stoppers are generally missing, which is another reason why they are cheap, so it's a good idea to buy up individual stoppers when you come across them – you rarely find one if you are looking specifically.

Get to know the difference between genuine cut glass and pressed glass. It's simple once you have seen the two together – and obviously it is the hand-cut glass which is really worth having. Pressed glass was introduced in the nineteenth century as a cheap substitute. The liquid glass was pressed in a mould to imitate the faceting of hand-cut glass, and was generally used for vinegar pourers or scent bottles. Occasionally there are silver necks or tops on these which make them valuable and some early pressed glass is now sought by collectors.

Junk glass can be bought and used for its original purposes – you could build up a mixed set of wine glasses, for example. Or you can improvise. Why not use an old-fashioned framed mirror as a table top? Old mirrors also make unusual trays. Glass vases and bottles are ideal for conversion to lamps, as are china vases and metal candlesticks (see pages 27–29).

Much old glass is beautiful enough to display. You may be lucky and come across something out of the ordinary like an election glass – a sort of nineteenth-century public relations gimmick with the favoured candidate's name engraved round the rim.

Nevertheless, don't just look for perfection. A less than perfect specimen can be restored to its former glory with practice and patience.

Cleaning

Just like china, junk glass may be greatly improved by thorough
cleaning. Dirt becomes ingrained in surface scratches and the
glass loses its shiny look. All the cleaning processes described
here can be applied to the interior as well as the exterior surface of the glass, and you will need to devise devious ways of
getting into some of the awkwardly shaped bottles and decanters. Try wrapping polishing cloths round old toothbrushes,
or using the ingenious brushes sold in music shops for cleaning wind instruments.

Cleaning Methods

1. *A proprietary glass polish* such as Windolene, or even a
metal polish like Goddards Silver Polish, will easily cope with
the average problem. Usually the scratches become invisible
once the dirt is out of them, and all you need do then is keep
the glass clean.

2. *Removing scratches:* if you're a perfectionist and the surface scratches still seem to be in evidence, then you can try to
get rid of the scratches themselves. To do this, take the polishing process one stage further. Glass is not the homogeneous hard
substance it appears. By rubbing it gently with an abrasive
polish like jewellers' rouge, you can smooth over the scratches.
You can buy a block of jewellers' rouge at a good ironmonger's
or a Do-It-Yourself store; apply it on a soft cloth, like polish.
If the surface doesn't respond satisfactorily to this treatment,
you can, as a last resort, varnish it with clear varnish to imitate
the right shiny appearance.

3. *Removing stains:* old glass containers frequently have
stains inside, such as wine or lime deposits. Soaking in a solution made by dissolving a 'Stainfree' tablet (from chemists or
hardware shops) in hot water will usually deal with these. Or
try soaking glass for a couple of days in pure distilled water
(you can buy this at the chemist's, drugstore, garage or filling
station) and scrubbing at the deposit with a baby's bottle brush
or the ever-useful toothbrush.

4. *Persistent stains* can be treated by the abrasive method.
Polish them with a mild abrasive like proprietary metal polish.

The chances are that the shape of the container will make it impossible to get at stains inside. In this case you can swill sand and warm water round to abrade the stain, shaking the container as if you were shaking a milk bottle.

5. *Cleaning with acid:* if none of these methods is successful, the stain has probably penetrated the glass. The discoloured layer will need to be burned off. To do this you should fill the container with a solution of some mild acid, such as vinegar and water – use two parts vinegar to one part water – or soak the whole article in a bowl of vinegar. Then wash it in warm detergent.

An old-fashioned remedy which is often successful is to soak the glass in warm water and ammonia. Begin by using a solution of equal parts and increase the strength if necessary. This is the best method for treating cloudiness (the result of prolonged exposure to damp conditions or a fume-laden atmosphere).

If you are really keen to restore a piece of glass which will not respond to home remedies, then you can take it to an expert – a glazier or a jeweller – who will burn off the skin of discoloured glass with strong acid. This is really better than experimenting with potentially dangerous acids yourself.

Removing Stoppers

A common problem with old glass bottles, decanters, vinegar pourers and such like is that the stoppers have become firmly wedged in. The worst thing to do is to try and force the stopper out – you will probably end up with a shattered bottle and the stopper jammed in the neck as firmly as ever. Be patient and try to ease the stopper out after lubricating it with some sort of oil or glycerine. Any lubricating agent will do, but if you have the ingredients to hand use a mixture of two parts pure alcohol – from the chemist's or drugstore – one part glycerine and one part table salt (a cupful should be more than enough). Paint the mixture where the stopper goes into the neck of the bottle, getting it as far down the sides as possible. Leave for a few hours and then try gently to remove the stopper. If you heat the bottle gently over a radiator or with a hairdryer, the expansion of the air inside may help to push the stopper out. But don't overheat the bottle and crack the glass.

Storage

Since glass, especially old glass, is very likely to become cloudy if it is exposed to damp conditions over a long period of time, you can save yourself a lot of bother by taking care over storage. Make sure glass is thoroughly dry inside and out before you pack it away. If it is a glass container with a lid or stopper, store the two pieces separately or you may trap moisture inside.

Mending

Riveting

Riveting is the old-fashioned way of mending glass. It is strong but unsightly and usually unnecessary nowadays because of the strength of modern adhesives. If you want to rivet glass, take it to an expert; your local glazier should be able to advise you.

Adhesives

Adhesives are the best way to mend broken glass. Follow exactly the method described for mending china on pages 16-19. Use either an epoxy resin like Araldite or one of the celluloid adhesives such as Durofix (the latter for pieces which are for display only). It's again important to use the minimum amount of glue and to tape the joins at right angles until they have set. Any excess glue which oozes from the join should be rubbed away with fine grade steel wool when it has set. Don't use glass/sand paper, which will scratch the glass.

Dowelling

Dowel repairs are another variation on the dowelling method used for wooden furniture and china and already described on pages 15-16. With glass, the method is most often used for mending the stems of drinking glasses, which aren't strong enough when mended with adhesive alone. A slim glass rod is inserted into the stem to strengthen it. Unfortunately most glasses have stems which are too narrow for anyone but an expert with fine equipment to cope with.

Unless the glass is very valuable indeed it will probably be too expensive to bother. All the same you may like to try your luck at home, on the wide stem of something like a glass goblet. The main thing to remember is to go slowly.

You should be able to buy a measured-off length of glass rod from your glass merchant to use as a dowel.

Using a very narrow bit on a hand drill, drill holes of equal depth into both halves of the broken stem. Insert the glass rod into the hole in the lower half of the stem, securing it with epoxy adhesive. Then cement the upper part of the stem into place. When the adhesive sets it will look a little cloudy but should not be unsightly.

A Chipped Rim

Grinding down the rim of a chipped glass or vase until the edge is smooth again can give good results if the chip is not too deep. You can do this at home if you are interested in lapidary work and own a grinding machine, or you can ask a glass merchant to do it for you.

Mirrors

The trouble with old mirrors is that very often they no longer do the job they were intended for, either because they are dirty or because the silvering on the back is wearing thin. RE-SILVERING is easily done by a local glass firm, though it can be expensive and may not be necessary if you bought the mirror essentially for its attractive frame. A real antique mirror may lose its value if re-silvered. If in doubt, take the mirror to a professional restorer.

A GOOD PROPRIETARY WINDOW CLEANER will do a lot for your mirror, but may not deal with the unfortunate problem of FLYMARKING. Flymarks can generally be removed with a solution of one part caustic soda to nineteen parts water. Be sure when applying this to wear strong rubber gloves, and if at all possible take the mirror outside. Wash the glass well afterwards and dry it thoroughly.

If the mirror is good but the frame is poor, you can re-frame it in something more attractive, using the methods described on pages 63–71.

Converting Bottles to Lamps

Although glass bottles are generally used for conversion to lamps, the same method can be applied to other containers – china vases, metal candlesticks, the sort of stone jars which used to hold cider and mineral waters (the best of these have the maker's name and advertising slogan on the front), are just a few of the possibilities.

1. Clean the container thoroughly and give it time to dry out thoroughly too (especially if it is glass) or you will get condensation inside the lamp.

2. Decide whether you want to hide the flex inside the container or whether you are going to let it show. This will depend largely on the type of container you are using, as if you decide to run it through the container you will need to drill an extra hole at the base to let the flex out again. It is more difficult to drill a hole successfully in glass or porcelain than, say, a stone jar, so in such cases an exterior flex would be best.

Lightweight containers have to be weighted down so that they don't topple over all the time. One of the favourite ways of doing this if you're using a clear glass container is to fill the bottle with coloured liquid. If you choose this method *it is not safe* to run a flex through the container (in any case the liquid might easily trickle through the exit hole). If you're anxious to hide the flex a better method of weighting down the bottle would be to use coloured sand or pebbles.

3. If you're going to run your flex through the bottle, drill a hole on the side at the base. Start with a small bit, and increase the size to enlarge the hole. Make sure the bottle is securely clamped before you start, so that it can't roll around. If you are converting a metal container such as a candlestick this exit hole must be covered with a rubber grummet to prevent the raw edges cutting through the flex.

4. You can buy from an electrical shop a switch/socket which will fit into the neck of the bottle. If the neck of the bottle is wider than the bulb socket it can be packed with fibre glass or plastic padding, to hold the socket firm. You can also buy sockets to use on solid articles such as blocks of wood. These are secured into position on the object. If possible, drill a hole through which to run the flex.

The switch/socket will have to be wired to a suitable length of flex, and of course you will need a plug for the other end of the flex. When wiring the flex to the switch/socket, remem-

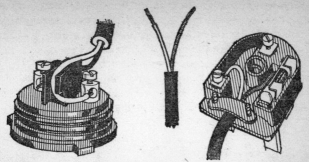

ber that brown is the live terminal, blue is the neutral, and green and yellow is the earth. (A lamp flex, however, does not always have an earth wire.) If the flex is to run through the bottle, thread it through *before* you fill the container with sand or pebbles.

5. You can cheer up plain bottles by covering them with a mosaic of small coloured stones. These stones (and the necessary cement) can be bought, already polished, from lapidary shops.

Enamel Repairs

Enamel looks like a type of china but in fact it's opaque glass fused on to a metal, such as copper. There used to be several famous enamelling factories in England, and one at Bilston has re-opened to re-create the craftsmanship of the Georgian period.

The two most common problems with old, and even modern, enamels, are dirt and the loosening of the enamel from its metal base.

Enamel is best cleaned with good soap and warm water, but don't soak it, and dry it thoroughly afterwards.

Unfortunately, as far as repairs are concerned, enamel cannot be re-fired, so you can't replace a missing section by the original method. However you *can* replace it with a reasonably convincing substitute. One possibility is the method described on pages 19–20 for repairing missing pieces of china – epoxy adhesive coloured with powder pigments from an artists'

29

supply shop. This can be varnished over with a clear varnish when dry, to give it an extra glazed effect. Art shops also sell kits for making brooches etc. from plastic imitation enamel which does not need to be fired. These can be used for minor repairs if you can get colours which match.

Alternatively, you can melt down coloured candles and use the warm soft wax. In many ways this is easier and gives a more natural effect, but it is less lasting and can collect dust.

Metals

Introduction

Junk metal ranges from the rusty iron base of a cheap oil lamp through brass fittings covered with thick gooey lacquer to tarnished silver on cut glass dressing table bottles. So renovating metal probably just means a thorough cleaning. First decide which metal you are dealing with. The most likely ones are brass, copper, iron, gold and silver; they are all described in this chapter. The junk may be 'plated' – that is, a thin coating of a more precious metal (often silver) has been applied to an article made of base metal.

Often clocks don't go simply because the metal mechanism is clogged with grime, and a good clean makes all the difference. There are several simple ways too of restoring the sparkle to jewellery.

Metal containers and candlesticks can be converted to lamps on the principles described on pages 27–29. Take care that the hole drilled for the flex is properly protected.

Cheap metal, or metal whose plating has worn thin, can be given a new lease of life with the liquid and wax preparations described on pages 98–99. These finishes are available in all the metallic colours from pewter to copper.

It's worth sorting through the boxes of cutlery which are always found at jumble sales and auctions, as there may be something of real value, either solid metal or plate. Many people collect Sheffield plate, which is copper plated with silver. Even when the plating of silver (which is thicker than the modern electro-plating) has worn through, the combination of copper and silver looks extremely attractive and would gain nothing from being restored and is best left alone after gentle cleaning.

GOLD

It has always seemed wrong to me that such an expensive metal should be so resistant to tarnishing and corrosion, but it is – think how well the treasures of Tutankhamun have lasted. Because of this, it's comparatively easy to restore gold to its original state.

Gold articles carry a hallmark to indicate the degree of fineness of the metal. Hallmarking was introduced in the fourteenth century to guarantee that the gold used in an artefact conforms to certain accepted standards. Most gold hallmarks consist of four symbols – indicating the assay office where the metal was tested, the maker of the article, the standard of the metal used, and the date. Over the six centuries it has been in force, there have been a lot of variations on this theme, but basically on a gold article you should look for a crown followed by a 'carat' figure to indicate the metal's degree of purity – pure gold is 24 carat. On present-day articles, this figure is 22, 18, 14 or 9.

Twenty-two carat gold is almost pure gold, with a little of another metal added to strengthen it. Nine carat gold is about thirty per cent pure gold, and since it contains the highest proportion of strengthening metal, it wears better than the purer alloys. If you have any real difficulty in getting gold to respond to the cleaning methods described here, then there is too much base metal in it, and you should try cleaning it with a solution of ammonia – one part ammonia to nine parts distilled water – as if it were brass or silver.

When you are cleaning and polishing gold, always avoid the hallmark as you need to keep this as sharp as possible.

If you would like to know more about hallmarks, there are several pocket-size books available.

Cleaning

A good wash in soap and water and a thorough drying with a soft cloth should be sufficient to cope with any surface tarnish. Use a soft paint brush or old toothbrush to get into the cracks and crannies.

Of the proprietary polishes, Goddards Long Term Silver Foam, which washes *and* shines the metal, is suitable. Of course all metal polishes are mildly abrasive and wear away a little metal every time they are used, so it is wise to avoid harsh remedies wherever possible, especially on a soft metal like gold.

Goddards anti-tarnish polishing cloths are mainly intended for silver but also prevent tarnish on gold. They should be used after washing and drying the metal.

Polishing

Scratches can be removed from gold with jewellers' rouge, which is available at good ironmongers' and Do-It-Yourself stores. It comes in a block and you use it on a soft cloth like a polish. Its abrasive action smooths down the surface, so you shouldn't overdo it.

A jeweller will generally re-burnish scratched gold quite cheaply.

Sterling silver is almost one hundred per cent pure metal with just enough alloy to strengthen it. Like gold it can be identified by its hallmark. Silver from London has a lion's head, and silver from Birmingham has an anchor. These are the most usual marks although there are others. Almost all Victorian silver has a very identifiable head of Queen Victoria stamped on it, in addition to the other marks, to show that duty has been paid on the article. The hallmark guides listed on page 114 will be useful if you like to know what you are buying. As with gold, you should avoid cleaning the hallmark.

In the eighteenth century a process for plating copper with silver was invented – the famous Sheffield plate already mentioned. In the nineteenth century electro-plating was invented: this is a process by which articles of base metal can be given a very thin coating of silver.

All the methods described are equally suitable for solid silver and plate unless specifically stated otherwise.

Cleaning

Because silver, like gold, is a very soft metal, always use a soft cloth, and however bad the tarnish don't get tempted to use drastic measures like Brillo pads.

1. *A good wash in warm soap and water* may be sufficient. Even if you have used another cleaning method a final wash and thorough drying is a good idea. If the washing isn't effective, there are several alternatives for removing tarnish and creating a really healthy shine.

2. *Proprietary polishes* are the simplest. Goddards make an excellent range. Their Long Term Silver Polish is good for silver and silver plate, and they also make their special Goddards Plate Powder, specifically for silver plate.

3. *Jewellers' rouge* has an abrasive effect which is good for removing tarnish, for eradicating scratches, and for producing a high shine. It should be applied with a soft brush or cloth.

4. *Ammonia solution* (about one part ammonia to nine parts distilled water) will remove tarnish if the article is soaked in

it. It will also stop mild corrosion if the article is left to soak for a couple of days. Ammonia has strong fumes and is best used out of doors or by an open window. Wear strong rubber gloves. Always be sure to wash ammonia (and any other chemical) off the article you are cleaning, and dry thoroughly. Otherwise any left-over traces will continue to eat into the metal.

This same solution can be used to treat tarnish on other metals.

On very stubborn patches of tarnish use a few drops of neat ammonia; then wash thoroughly.

5. *Chemical cleaners* are ideal for treating silver which is heavily decorated or embossed. If you use a proprietary cleaner on embossed silver, it's impossible to clean all the polish out of the cracks, and the residue dries there, leaving an ugly film. Goddards make a chemical cleaner called Silver Dip, which brings articles up very well.

Alternatively you can take silver objects to a jeweller and ask him to send them away to be dipped in cyanide. This removes a thin skin of metal and exposes fresh bright metal underneath. Not many jewellers do this on the premises as a special licence is needed for the cyanide.

6. *The aluminium method* is old-fashioned, but it is still a very effective way of removing tarnish from silver. Place some

scraps of aluminium (baking foil is ideal) in an enamelled bowl or sink. Fill the bowl with boiling water and washing soda (two tablespoonfuls of washing soda to half a litre or $2\frac{1}{2}$ cupfuls of water). Place the silver in the bowl and after a good deal of frothing and fizzing the tarnish will disappear. Remove the silver articles. Rinse them in clean, warm water and dry them.

Preventing Tarnish and Corrosion

When you've cleaned your silver you will want to prevent the same problem recurring. You could varnish the silver with clear varnish to prevent this, but it's not really very satisfactory as it tends to make the silver look like a cheaper metal. The important thing is to keep silver away from the conditions that cause tarnish and corrosion. Damp air, and especially damp *sea* air, should be avoided. (The salt in the sea air reacts with the copper used to harden the silver and causes it to corrode.) Chemical pollution in town air may also result in corrosion. You must also prevent silver coming into contact with ordinary household salt (it is to prevent this happening that silver salt and pepper sets have a blue glass lining). Black plastic bags keep out moisture and obviously silver must not be kept in a steamy kitchen.

Goddards and Town Talk make polishing cloths which bring up a good shine and which are impregnated with a substance which prevents tarnish. They should be used after the silver has been washed. These cloths will not remove tarnish once it has occurred.

Restoring Silver

1. Scratches can be removed by applying jewellers' rouge on a soft cloth. Follow this up by a polish with swansdown rouge (from a hardware shop) which is not as harsh as jewellers' rouge.

2. Since silver is very soft, minor bumps and dents can be gently knocked back into shape with a rubber hammer, or even pressed back into shape by hand.

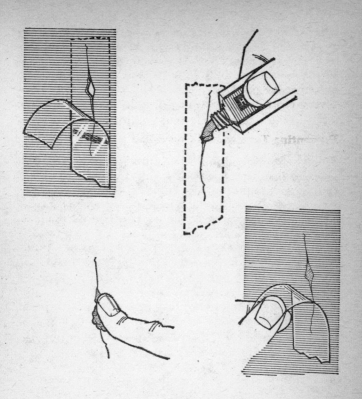

3. You can cover over cracks and holes to improve the article's appearance – but not if the join has to take any strain. Use plastic padding from an ironmonger's or try the epoxy putty used for filling cracks in china. This is a gooey substance which you can use to fill in cracks or holes; build it up and then leave it to harden. The effect is rather cheap, but it works very well if you are going to use a metallic paint or wax to finish off the article (as described on pages 98–99). If you are trying to fill a wide gap, you should stick masking tape underneath the hole, on the wrong side, and build up the new surface on top of that.

4. If you need to stick metal to metal, use epoxy adhesive, although success can't be guaranteed.

5. Broken silver can be soldered back together again, but this requires a soldering iron and considerable practice in using it. Do not use soft solder, as the lead in it will cause corrosion. Your local jeweller may be able to recommend someone to do soldering for you.

6. Worn silver plate can sometimes be re-plated, although you may find difficulty in getting small items accepted. Ask your jeweller if he knows of a local firm which specialises in plating.

7. If you have a piece of silver plate on which the plating has worn thin, or if you have a metal article you would like to make look like silver, you can use the products described on pages 98–99. Remember to clean the surface thoroughly, removing any traces of a previous finish. If you use silver wax, it will definitely need to be lacquered over to achieve the correct appearance. Liquid 'Treasure Leaf' gives a simple and convincing silver finish.

COPPER AND BRASS

Copper is a pure metal; brass is an alloy of copper and zinc. Both can be treated in more or less the same way.

Cleaning

The same proprietary cleaners are used for copper and brass: for example, Goddards Brass Polish, Goddards Copper Polish, Duraglit Wadding, and Royal Normandy which washes *and* shines.

A paint-remover, such as Polystrippa, will get rid of paint and varnish.

A mild acid, such as lemon juice or vinegar mixed with salt, works well on light tarnish. It should be applied on a soft cloth. Really bad green tarnish can be treated with rust remover painted on with a brush. Wash off acid or rust remover very thoroughly, or left-over traces will continue to eat into the metal.

The ammonia solution recommended for silver – one part

ammonia to nine parts distilled water – is an effective cleaner for brass and copper as well. It's particularly good for removing traces of grease.

After treating the metal with paint remover, acid or ammonia, bring up the shine by using a proprietary polish. Brass articles are often of a rather elaborate design, either because they are of oriental workmanship or because they were intended to be decorative – horse brasses, for instance.

The cracks and crevices can be cleaned with a paintbrush or an old toothbrush. Another problem occurs when you want to clean decorative brass fittings on something like a grandfather clock or a writing box. If at all possible, the brass fittings should be removed, and replaced once cleaned. If this is impossible, the adjacent surfaces should be protected with masking tape.

Restoring

Copper and brass don't look too bad if they are lacquered to prevent tarnish, and this certainly saves a lot of cleaning time, particularly if items are to be kept in a damp atmosphere – a kitchen or a bathroom. Use a clear metal varnish like Rustins.

There are metallic paints and waxes both in brass and copper colours, described on page 98. The paints and lacquers give a shinier finish which looks more authentic, especially for the brass. These are also useful for renovating a brass or copper 'finish' which is wearing away so that the base metal shows through.

Fire-irons, fenders or cheap country oil lamps are the type of iron junk which you can adapt for use in your home. Iron rusts easily and, since it is brittle, it is often broken. Rust occurs when the metal is exposed to damp conditions. If you want to avoid the same thing happening after you have restored it, keep the article in a dry atmosphere and protect it with a decorative finish or a clear lacquer like Rustins.

Cleaning

After the care needed in dealing with soft metals, there is a good deal of satisfaction to be had from adopting more brutal methods with rusty iron. Even stubborn rust responds to a Brillo pad used under running water. You can also use the sort of strong rust remover which is made for car bodywork. This may also prevent rust recurring. A toothbrush, or better still a small wire brush, will be useful for getting into awkward corners.

Paint and lacquer come off with a paint remover like Polystrippa.

Restoring

When the rust, old paint and old lacquer have been removed, you may wish to paint the metal or to give it a different metallic finish. Before deciding to do this, do pause and consider whether it looks better as it is. Sometimes an oil lamp, which has a certain charm when the base is cleaned up and there are traces of old gilding in the embossing, can look horribly vulgar with a new coat of synthetic gold.

Possible finishes are listed below:

1. Iron usually takes very well to all the methods of imitation gilding, and looks good in any of the colours. A pewter-coloured finish is often a good choice if you have a large surface to cover, as it is less aggressive than some of the colours. Or you could just pick out the raised patterning in Liquid Leaf (page 98).

2. Household paint is easy to apply to iron and gives you a completely different range of colours. Prepare the iron for painting with a metal primer.

3. Plastic padding or epoxy putty described on page 37 work quite well on iron if the repair isn't intended to take any strain.

4. If a piece of brittle iron has snapped, the sharp edges can be filed down with a metal file.

5. You can stick metal to metal with epoxy adhesive, although the results are not always reliable.

OTHER PROJECTS

Hinges and Locks

Hinges and locks are normally made of iron, though they can be made of another metal such as brass. If locks are stiff and rusty they can often be restored to working order by a heavy soaking in light oil, the sort used for squeaky doors.

Beardmores make locks in a wide variety of patterns, and copies of old-style locks. They can also supply a wide variety of standard spare keys. This is very useful since boxes and chests are worth far more if they can be locked. Their catalogue can be obtained from J. D. Beardmore & Co. Ltd, 3–5 Percy Street, London W1.

Hinges, like locks, respond to a good oiling.

Where the pin is missing from the hinge you can sometimes improvise successfully with a nail or length of wire a little larger than the original pin. Slip this through the back of the hinge and bend the narrow end over to prevent its falling out.

Oil Lamps

The base of an oil lamp is of metal. The best and most expensive have a brass base, but you will be very lucky indeed to find one of these in a junk shop. The later models often have a cast iron base, which was painted or given an imitation gold or silver finish.

There is also a metal fitting where the bowl joins the base. This is generally brass, even on the cheaper models, but if it is not, the finish may need touching up with metallic paint.

The bowl which contains the oil can be of glass or china, and should be cleaned accordingly. Before you use an oil lamp it's a wise precaution to fill this bowl with water and leave it in the sink overnight to discover whether it has a slow – or even a fast – leak.

Screwed into the top of the bowl is the metal wick regulator. This enables you to turn the cloth wick up or down and adjust the light. Some oil lamps have a double wick; and while ordinary oil lamps merely have a simple chimney which fits round the wick and protects the flame, double-wicked ones also have a glass bowl to reflect the light. All these components can still be bought separately. You may be lucky enough to find an original piece from an old lamp; alternatively you can get modern ones. These are still being made, and the recent vogue for imitation brass oil lamps has made it much easier to get the spare parts.

When you have restored an oil lamp, varnish the metal parts with clear metal varnish. If you don't, the oil and smoke will make frequent cleaning and polishing necessary.

Clocks

Unless you are extraordinarily mechanically minded, most of your clock repairs will have to go to an expert. However, there are some things which can be tried before committing yourself to vast expense.

For example, if your clock has an over-loud chime, try bending the hammer back a little so that it strikes more gently on the bell.

Pendulum clocks, like grandfather clocks and cuckoo clocks, may be fast or slow merely because they're not exactly level or because the pendulum may need adjusting to the right length. On some clocks this can be done very simply by sliding the weight up and down the pendulum in a hit and miss fashion until you find the correct length. The higher up the pendulum you push the weight, the faster the clock will go. If the weight isn't adjustable you will have to get a new pendulum cut to length.

Cleaning

The simplest and most obvious way you can help your clock is by cleaning it. Protect all the non-mechanical bits with newspaper or polythene, remembering to cover up any areas on to which the cleaning fluids may drip. Then paint paraffin on to the mechanism. This will dissolve the grime. Most of the paraffin will run away or evaporate, but you can wipe it off the less fragile areas with a clean brush.

Afterwards lightly oil the working parts (the gears and the springs) using a good quality clock oil, applied with a thin paintbrush. Ask a clockmaker for advice about possible oils.

Three-in-One is suitable for most ordinary clocks, but there are special oils for particularly fragile parts. Over-oiling is a mistake as dust and dirt will stick to the oil and clog up the works again.

A useful tip for keeping dirt out of long-case clocks is to line them inside with brown paper.

Directions on how to clean the wooden parts, and the decorative metal and enamel parts, of the clock are given in the appropriate chapters.

Jewellery

Means of cleaning gold and silver have already been described on pages 33–36.

If you want to clean a RING, first check whether the stones are in a claw setting or, like much old jewellery, simply stuck in with adhesive.

Claw-set rings can be dipped into methylated spirit; if you want to avoid dipping the stone, the methylated spirit can be applied with a brush. *Check the comments on specific stones below.* Any cracks and filigree can be cleaned out with a soft brush in the same way.

Stones stuck in with adhesive are less secure than claw settings and such rings should be worked on with a soft brush dipped into methylated spirit. Rub the ring afterwards with a soft rag to bring up the shine.

DIAMONDS, if in a secure claw setting, can be treated by a wash in soapy water followed by a rinsing. This will also benefit the metal. Bring back the sparkle by brushing the diamond with a little surgical spirit (you can buy this from the chemist's), and dry it.

Other stones are less sturdy, and shouldn't be submitted to anything more drastic than lukewarm water and soapsuds. Don't wash stones like this unless they are in a secure setting.

OPALS AND TURQUOISES SHOULD NEVER BE PUT IN WATER.

Goddards Jewellery Care Kit is a proprietary cleaner which

is suitable for metal settings, precious stones, and even pearls. It really does get at the accumulated dirt. The kit consists of a dip, a brush and a polish.

CHIPPED CAMEOS, JET MOURNING JEWELLERY, AMBER AND CORAL can be mended with epoxy adhesive mixed with the appropriate colour, as described on page 19–20. They will all respond very well to a wash in lukewarm soapy water.

Missing stones can be replaced by the jeweller – with real stones if you can afford it, and with paste stones if you can't. Alternatively, you can buy stones and adhesive from a lapidary shop and do the job yourself.

Paintings, Prints, Books and Papier Mâché

Introduction

Watercolours, prints and books deteriorate rapidly when kept in conditions that are too dry or too humid. Extreme conditions will also affect leather book bindings, making them brittle and flaky or encouraging mould. You should therefore check regularly, especially if you have central heating. It's possible to buy an electric humidifier to counteract the drying-out effects of central heating. Alternatively, you can put down small dishes of water. These precautions will benefit oil paintings and wooden furniture as well, and prevent them from cracking or veneer from lifting.

Be careful to hang your pictures and shelve your books in a suitable part of the room. They should be against a dry, preferably an inside, wall, and away from the damaging effects of direct sunlight. Watercolours especially fade very easily. If you hang pictures over a radiator or fire you risk damaging them by drying out the paper, the adhesive in the frame and backing and, in the case of oil paintings, the pigment itself.

Air must be allowed to circulate round books and pictures. It is a mistake to put books in a glass-fronted bookcase which prevents this, and which encourages insects to feel secure and undisturbed. If you have a good closed bookcase it would be better used for displaying china or glass and cutting down the necessity for all that boring dusting. It can be easily 'converted' for this by lining the shelves with velvet in a colour which will set your possessions off to good effect.

You can still get lots of interesting things to decorate your walls very easily and very cheaply (compare the prices of old paintings and prints with the price of a glossy reproduction 'Old Master' from a chain store). If you can't see a print which you like, take a look inside an old book and see what you can find. Old books are very often used as a source by specialist

46

shops. Plain black and white prints can be lightly tinted with watercolours if they need brightening up and this will make them look twice as expensive. But make sure, *before* you begin enthusiastically on the ripping apart process, that you aren't ruining a really good book.

Rather ordinary, but still pleasant, watercolours are common – usually rustic views done by enthusiastic amateurs in the days when art was considered a necessary accomplishment. It isn't quite so easy to find leather-bound books in good condition, the dealers usually get there first. I have known them go to quite insignificant jumble sales the day before the event and take away the best for a lump sum. All the same, if you are not too interested in what the book is about, you can soon acquire a shelf-ful of beautiful if rather tedious volumes.

Papier mâché is often mistaken for wood because of its texture and because it is frequently made into quite substantial articles, like tables. Despite its deceptive appearance it should be treated with care as it is easily damaged by hot liquids.

COLOUR-FAST PRINTS

Cleaning

Every time you treat paper you weaken it slightly so it's best to start with the least drastic cleaning measures and only then, if the results are still not tolerable, move on to more complex methods, such as bleaching. Where staining is very marked it's unlikely you will be able to get perfect results – but after all, many people like to see at least some evidence of age in prints.

Before you start make sure you have plentiful supplies of *clean* white blotting paper and a fairly large piece of plate glass to support the paper if you are going to use any of the soaking methods.

These methods can only be applied safely to colour-fast prints (which watercolours, for instance, are not). If you are in doubt, test a small area at the edge of the print *before* plunging joyfully for the tap or the solvent.

Surface Marks and Grease

Some marks may not have penetrated the paper but can be rubbed off the surface with *an eraser*. Don't use a harsh rubber but a soft gum eraser, like the large yellow erasers obtainable from art shops, which won't tear the paper. An alternative is to rub the paper with soft (but not too fresh) white bread-crumbs. This method is most effective when the marks are slightly greasy – fingerprints, for example. The bread absorbs the grease, as well as having a mildly abrasive effect. As soon as the bread begins to look the least bit grubby throw it away and start afresh.

More serious grease marks require a more radical treatment – *a grease solvent*. This should be applied sparingly to the marks on swabs of cotton wool. The most obvious grease solvent is pure petrol but it's best to avoid using this because it is so highly inflammable ('flammable' is an alternative term). Benzene and Benzole are recommended for removing grease stains from paper. They are also inflammable so take care if you decide to try them, and don't use them anywhere near a naked flame.

A non-inflammable (or 'non-flammable') solvent is carbon tetrachloride, the major ingredient of most proprietary spot removers, like Thawpit and Dabitoff. Although it isn't in-flammable the fumes can be dangerous over a period of time, and it's preferable to work outside or at least with the windows open.

If you prefer to avoid any problems like this, particularly if there are young children around, then the old-fashioned method of *ironing up* the grease may be best. To do this place

the print between two sheets of clean white blotting paper and iron with a warm iron. If the print seems very fragile, hold the iron just above the blotting paper. The heat will melt the grease which will be soaked up by the blotting paper. That, at least, is the theory; it works better on some substances, particularly wax, than it does on others.

When using a solvent or when using the ironing method you can help to prevent the stain spreading over a wider area of the paper by damping round it before you start.

Removing Stubborn Stains and Foxing

'Foxing' is the name given to the brown splodgy stains which frequently discolour old paper. It is usually associated with the musty smell of old books. This musty smell and the discoloration of the paper are the result of damp conditions which encourage a fungus to grow on the paper. This causes the brown (or even sometimes black) stains which, because they are living fungi, spread very rapidly. Other stains which often need similar treatment are ink stains, and patches and streaks of the old glue which was used for mounting prints and watercolours.

There are several points to remember when attempting the 'wet' methods of treating these stains. The methods sound quite easy but in practice there are several pitfalls which make it unwise to attempt them on anything of great value.

You will certainly need plenty of clean white blotting paper.

If you are going to bleach the print, then remember that most bleaches cause vapours and it is best to work with a window open. When washing or bleaching paper *don't* put it in a container and then pour the liquid on to it; the pressure of the liquid on one particular area may cause it to disintegrate. First fill the container, then immerse the paper.

Finally, it's a good idea to have a sheet of plate glass or polythene to support the paper while it's in the water. You needn't then handle the paper while it is wet. Instead just pick up the piece of glass it is lying on.

The dishes sold in photographic supply shops for developing prints make good containers for washing and bleaching.

1. *Soaking* in cold distilled water (from the chemist's or drugstore, or the garage) may be sufficient for some stains,

though not for foxing. Immerse the print, on its glass sheet, in a dish full of distilled water. When it looks clean, remove it from the water. Don't attempt to take the paper off the glass immediately, instead place a piece of clean blotting paper lightly over it. When the print is beginning to dry out, turn it over on to the blotting paper as if you were turning a cake out of a tin and place another piece of blotting paper on top of it.

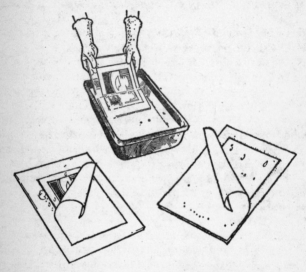

2. *A weak solution of a Teepol-based detergent such as Stergene* – that is, approximately a quarter the strength recommended on the bottle – may be necessary if distilled water isn't enough to treat the stains. Again, remember to support the paper on a sheet of glass or polythene and to immerse it in a ready-filled container.

Rinse the print by immersing it in a second container, this time full of cold distilled water; then dry it according to the instructions given under *Soaking*. It is most important not to neglect the rinsing, as any left-over traces of soap will encourage new fungus growths.

Soaking in clear water or Stergene solution should be

sufficient to remove any old glue which you want to clean off the back of a picture before re-mounting.

3. *Bleaching* will usually remove stubborn stains and foxing. The easiest method is to immerse the print in a solution of sodium hypochlorite (Milton) or hydrogen peroxide; follow the maker's instructions, and begin with a moderately strong solution, increasing the strength gradually if necessary. Afterwards rinse it in cold distilled water.

Another good bleach for paper is Chloramine T, which is available from a chemist's shop or drugstore. Make up half a litre (2½ cupfuls) in the proportions of about one part Chloramine T to fifty parts cold distilled water.

4. *Isolated patches* of discoloration (typical of foxing which is caught in time) can be treated without immersing the whole print. Instead you can paint a solution of hydrogen peroxide or sodium hypochlorite (Milton) on to each individual spot.

Use a soft brush, place the print on clean white blotting paper to soak up anything which comes through and blot up the bleach with more clean blotting paper. Rinse by brushing with distilled water, which should then be blotted up.

This method avoids weakening the print unnecessarily with continuous soakings.

Re-sizing

Re-sizing may be necessary, as soakings will make the print progressively limper by removing the original size – that is, the substance used to stiffen and glaze the paper. If the paper becomes really floppy then you can give it back its 'body' by dipping it into a solution of 15 grammes gelatine to four and a half litres of water (or 1 level tablespoon to 20 cupfuls), as if you were starching it.

Let the print dry thoroughly on clean blotting paper.

Ironing

You can smooth out creased prints by ironing them. If you've used any of the soaking methods the print will definitely need to be ironed.

Place the print on clean white blotting paper; put a sheet of clean brown paper over it to prevent scorching; and use a warm iron. If the print is still creased, sprinkle the blotting paper with a little water, and iron again.

Mildew

Mildew thrives in damp conditions. It can be brushed off paper. It's particularly likely to occur where prints and water-colours have been mounted with glues, such as Scotch Glue or flour-and-water paste, made from organic materials.

Sterilising

The glue also encourages foxing. Obviously, when you've been to the trouble of getting rid of foxing stains, you will want to avoid having to deal with them again. To prevent them you will have to sterilise the paper and the simplest way to do so is to use Thymol Solution (one part sterilising powder to nineteen parts water) or a proprietary mixture from the chemist's. You can either apply this direct to the affected area or, if there is any possibility of liquid damaging the picture, you can soak a backing sheet in the solution and, when it has dried, place it behind the picture in the frame.

You should also remove any traces of the old glue which was the root of the trouble. If you can't scrape it away, use one of the soaking methods described earlier in this chapter.

WATERCOLOURS AND NON-FAST PRINTS

Watercolours, prints in non-fast inks and tinted prints cannot be subjected to *all* the above treatments because the colours will run. Unfortunately they are just as liable to get discoloured and to be spotted by foxing. If the picture isn't over-valuable then it may be worth treating the individual patches of stain-ing by the methods described under point 4, and afterwards treating it with a sterilising solution. Otherwise it must be taken to expert restorers.

Oil paintings are totally different from watercolours and prints and have to be treated totally differently. A canvas basically consists of linen primed with a mixture of glue and gesso so that the oil paints won't rot the fabric. The canvas is then stretched taut on a frame. The oil paints are various pigments ground up in linseed and poppyseed oil. When the painting is complete, it is varnished over to protect it.

There are a multitude of things which can go wrong with an oil painting because it is so complex. It's quite common to see the paint flaking and splitting and the priming layer showing through, particularly if the painting is hung in a centrally-heated room. This is because the layers of primer and paint are drying out – and drying out at different rates, since they are dissimilar substances. This sort of problem is strictly for the experts. So too are repairs to the canvas and re-backing. The only element which the amateur can tackle without risking too much damage is the varnish layer, and even this must be done with great caution. In your zeal to clean the varnish you can easily clean off the entire painting. The usual problem is that the protective varnish is dirty or cloudy and is fulfilling its protective function to such an extent that it obscures the picture itself.

Cleaning the Varnish

1. If the varnish seems only slightly dull, a proprietary varnish cleaner obtainable from an art shop may brighten it considerably.

2. Heavier grease and dirt can be removed with white spirit, applied very sparingly. Whatever you do *don't* slosh it on, or the whole process will quickly run away with you and you will have a blank canvas – which is taking cleanliness a bit too far.

Stripping and Re-varnishing

Even after cleaning the varnish may look dull. If the painting is a nineteenth-century one this may be the result of deliberate darkening to make it look like an old master. Dull and discoloured varnish must be stripped off and the painting re-varnished with a modern synthetic varnish which won't turn yellow with age.

This again is really a job for the expert but if the painting isn't particularly valuable you may like to have a go yourself. Common solvents used on varnishes are pure alcohol (from the chemist's or drugstore) and acetone. Apply the solvent very carefully, on a wad of clean linen. Alcohol and acetone work very fast, and alcohol will dissolve oil as well as varnish, so take great care. If things start to run away with you, apply an 'antidote': kerosene for acetone, turpentine for alcohol.

It's always wise to test first on the edge of the painting which is usually hidden by the frame.

When the old varnish has been cleaned off, apply a modern varnish. There are several different makes and they can be bought at any artists' supply shop.

Removing Damp 'Bloom'

Damp conditions produce a dull 'bloom' on the surface of a painting. This may mean stripping off all the varnish and refinishing, as just described. Before you give yourself the bother of doing so, however, try gently polishing the varnish with a soft cloth and a very good quality wax polish, such as Renaissance Wax. This may restore the shiny surface. Whatever you do, avoid leaving the painting in damp conditions where the problem will occur again.

BOOKS

Cleaning the Pages

To a large extent the marks and stains on books can be treated by the methods described for prints on pages 47–52, but with obvious limitations – you can't soak the whole book, especially if it has a leather cover. The best results are achieved by being patient and treating each mark or stain separately.

The edges of the pages are more likely to be dusty than anything else. They can be dusted, then cleaned with white breadcrumbs (not too fresh, but soft) or an artist's soft gum eraser; if they are gilded, be careful in case you start to rub the gilding away. Pencil marks and other minor blemishes on the pages can be erased in the same way.

Greasy finger marks are more common in books than on prints; here again, breadcrumbs may be sufficient to absorb all the grease. If not, you will have to use a grease solvent, as described on page 48. Apply it sparingly on wads of cotton wool.

Sometimes grease and wax can be blotted up by ironing the page with a warm iron, between sheets of clean white blotting paper.

Foxing stains have already been described on page 49. These and other stubborn stains, like ink, will have to be treated by bleaching with a solution of sodium hypochlorite (Milton) or hydrogen peroxide. Follow the instructions on page 51. Again, each stain will need to be treated separately. Rinse by brushing with cold distilled water. Use clean blotting paper to blot up the bleach and the distilled water used for rinsing, and protect the rest of the pages with more clean blotting paper, to prevent marks going through.

Foxing often results in the pages being stuck together. If this is the case, you will have to steam them apart – being careful not to *tear* them apart. Make sure your hands are protected from the steam. The pages should then be interleaved with clean white blotting paper and allowed to dry. When they are thoroughly dry, iron each one with a warm iron, first protecting the page with a surface layer of brown paper.

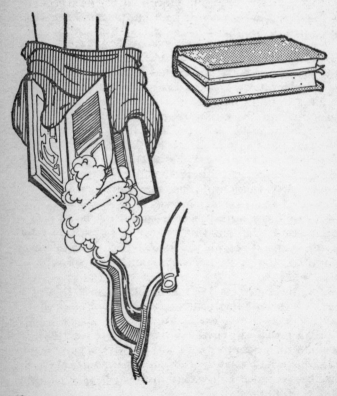

Cleaning Leather Bindings

Greasy marks on leather bindings should be removed by soaking up the grease (this is on the same principle as the breadcrumb treatment for greasy paper). To do this, cover the leather with fuller's earth (you can buy this from the chemist or drugstore). If you can't get fuller's earth, use talcum powder. Leave it on for about an hour and then brush it off. You'll have to treat each board and the spine separately. If there is a particularly difficult grease stain, try rubbing it gently with a little proprietary stain remover like Dabitoff, which contains carbon tetrachloride.

Other stains may respond to an application of oil of eucalyptus (from any chemist's or drugstore) on a wad of cotton wool, followed by treatment with fuller's earth.

Remember that the leather is often paper thin, so don't apply any great pressure to get rid of stains.

When the binding is as clean as you can get it, give it a polish with a good quality wax polish like Renaissance Wax or Goddards Cabinet Wax. To keep the binding supple you should re-polish it from time to time, but always *avoid any gilding* as this will rub off.

Renovating

Mending Torn Pages

You're most likely to want to stick in pages or mend torn pages, and for this Sellotape is simple and efficient. The fewer mendings you do the better, however, since every time you stick them together you make the book a little thicker than it was meant to be, and eventually it will no longer lie flat.

Joins which are going to take any strain should be mended with the strongest Sellotape. The point at which the book's bound-together pages are joined to the end-papers, which in turn are joined to the cover boards, takes the greatest strain. If you are joining the end-papers, or even the cover boards themselves, to the book's first or last page, leave a little 'hinge' of Sellotape free so that there is enough play left for the book to be opened and closed easily. A detached spine or an endpaper which has come away from the cover boards should be stuck down with any adhesive suitable for paper, and any excess wiped away immediately.

One of the disadvantages of Sellotape is that it tends to look yellow on the page. To avoid this problem and make the join match as nearly as possible, you could make your own gummed strip. Do this by cutting long narrow strips of paper which is as close as possible to the colour of the original paper. Paste these on one side (preferably with white paste or the paste used by photographers for mounting pictures) and use them as you would use strips of Sellotape. Obviously they can only be used for sticking the bound pages to the end-papers or cover boards, or where you run no risk of obscuring the print.

If it is going to be difficult to see the print through the Sellotape – and especially if your repair might obscure some delicate line illustration – an alternative, though not as strong as Sellotape, is Butterfly Tape. The disadvantage of Butterfly Tape is that you have to damp it on the gummy side and it quickly becomes unstickable if it gets too wet.

Mending Torn and Cracked Leather
A leather binding which is holed or torn can be patched with special leather from art shops. Be sure to get this special leather as it is very thin and prepared especially for the purpose.

Tidy up the tear with a pair of sharp scissors. Using tracing paper, trace the outline of the hole. This is your template. Cut a patch from the new leather, making it fractionally larger than the template. Make sure there is no dirt or grease on the cover which would prevent the glue taking effect. Smear a little glue on to the wrong side of the patch and fix it into position, tucking the edges down under the old leather. Weight the repair with some heavy books and leave to dry.

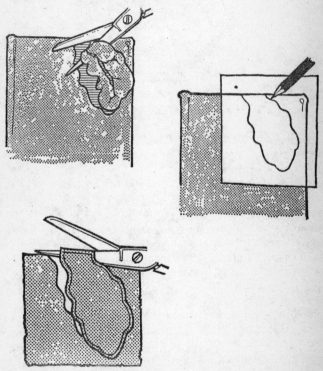

If the leather is dry and cracked, dress it liberally with saddle soap, following the instructions on the tin. This will go a long way to restoring its condition. Unfortunately, once the leather has started to flake, which it usually does on the corners, it is beyond repair.

Gilding

With the pages mended and the leather restored you can go one stage further and re-vitalise any gilding – either round the edges of the pages or on the leather itself. For the edges of the pages use gilt wax (described on page 98). Wedge the book tightly so that you have a smooth surface to work on, then rub the wax on with a finger. When this has been done, the wax can be polished to a shine with a soft cloth.

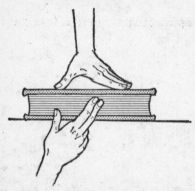

You can also paint on liquid gold (this is also described on page 98), but if you do, be sure that the pages are wedged together as tightly as possible or it will run into the print; and protect the covers with old polythene bags. If you are using gilding preparations of this kind, you will need to take special precautions, so check the instructions on the tin, and read the section on page 98 first.

You can try gold transfer foil (a sort of gold carbon paper) available from art shops, if you want to print titles and authors' names on to leather covers, where the original lettering has worn thin.

Fumigating

Books are often attacked by insects. The most common are woodworm (described more fully on page 74), silver fish and booklice. As soon as you see any signs of infestation *all* the suspect books should be isolated and then fumigated. To fumigate, you will need an airtight box, cotton wool and a vermifuge such as carbon disulphide or the proprietary brand, Insectrol. You can buy carbon disulphide from a chemist's or drugstore, and Insectrol is available at Do-It-Yourself shops and ironmongers'.

Line the box with cotton wool which has been impregnated with vermifuge according to the maker's instructions. Insert the book, cover it with more impregnated cotton wool, and put on the lid. Leave it for a day or so. Don't be put off by the smell, which will eventually wear off when the book is back in the fresh air.

You can discourage infestation by keeping the books where the air can circulate round them, and dusting them frequently.

PAPIER MÂCHÉ

Papier Mâché is frequently found in the form of trays or small lacquered tables on bamboo legs. It was very popular in the nineteenth century. The two most likely problems with papier mâché are woodworm and gaps where lumps have been broken off.

Woodworm

To treat woodworm, follow the instructions given on pages 74–76.

Replacing Missing Pieces

Missing sections can be replaced by making up some more papier mâché on the principles still used in primary schools. Soak a torn-up newspaper in water overnight (the pieces should be quite finely shredded). Drain off the excess water and mix the newspaper with a flour-and-water paste to make a malleable pulp. Use the pulp to fill the gap, over-packing it to allow for shrinkage when the water dries out. Any excess can be sanded down when dry.

An alternative method is to use the mixture described on pages 19–20 for mending china – epoxy adhesive mixed with titanium dioxide or a proprietary filler like Barbola paste. Again, remember to over-fill, and sand down any excess when the new section is dry.

When the repair is completed paint or lacquer it to match the original. You will probably need black lacquer for most designs.

Frames

Introduction

You may wish to restore a junk frame, still keeping the original picture, or you might prefer to adapt the frame for a different picture. Old frames are generally well made, are wood not plastic and can give family photographs a more individual look than a photographer's standard mount. If you make pictures from pressed flowers or needlework an old-fashioned frame is ideal. Oil paintings, however, must be sent to a professional framer.

Look out for Oxford frames. Their corners are not mitred but overlap to form a cross.

Look out too for oval and circular frames, and frames carved with fruit and flowers. Besides using them for their original purposes, you can easily make an unusual mirror by framing a piece of mirror glass, cut to fit by the glazier.

Adapting and mending frames offers a useful opportunity for you to try out on a small scale the methods of treating wood described in the next chapter – and especially techniques like gilding, which really do require a bit of practice.

Do bear in mind while re-framing that it isn't just a question of getting something that looks good, but also, where prints, watercolours and needlework are concerned, of keeping the dust and dirt out.

A picture will last better if the air can circulate freely round it. So, when you have finished re-framing, stick a small square of cork on the back near the lower edge of the frame, to prevent its hanging completely flush with the wall.

Cleaning, Mending and Re-finishing

Tackle cleaning, mending and re-finishing in the following stages.

1. *Dismantling.* If you are using an old frame for re-framing a different picture it will have to be totally dismantled. Even if you are using the original picture the frame will probably need a good clean, which can only be done thoroughly by taking the whole thing apart.

As you take the frame apart make a note of the component parts and check whether any of them will need to be replaced. Re-framing is simply a common-sense matter of putting the pieces back together in the right order.

Starting from the back you will first find a layer of brown paper stuck down with gummed strip, which is there to tidy the frame up and keep out the dirt.

Next is a stiff backing either of card or hardboard, which is kept in position by tacks knocked into the frame at an angle. Bend the tacks back carefully, and with any luck you'll be able to use the same tacks when you replace the backing board. Check the backing board for signs of woodworm – if there are any tell-tale holes it will have to be replaced with a new piece.

After the backing board comes the print, mounted on a piece of card or stiff paper (often another old picture). If the print is smaller than the frame the mount may be coloured to set the picture off, or, alternatively, there will be a card or paper frame set between the picture and the glass.

Between the glass and the outer wooden frame there is often an inner frame, consisting of four strips of mitred wood, usually gilded. This, like the coloured mount or the card frame, is there to set the picture off to advantage.

The glass itself fits exactly into the rebates of the outer frame.

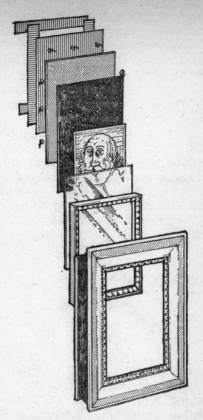

2. *Cleaning.* The first step is to clean the component parts as well as possible. The wooden parts of the frame can be washed with warm soapy water; be careful not to loosen any glued joints.

Use a proprietary window cleaner on both sides of the glass, and if it's still greasy, wipe it over with a rag dipped in methylated spirit.

The picture itself may need to be cleaned. If it is stained or if you want to remove it from its original mount and clean off the old glue, follow one of the methods described on pages 50–51.

3. *Repairing*. When everything is clean, carry out any repairs which are necessary. If the glass is broken or cracked, get your glass merchant to cut a new piece to size (it should fit exactly into the grooves on the inside of the frame). Remember to ask for the special *lightweight picture glass*.

The nails may be missing from the corners of the frame, or the glue may have come unstuck; these will need to be repaired. Epoxy adhesive is probably the best way of doing this, even if nails were used before. Remove any broken nails or old glue and clean the edges which are to be glued together, wiping them with a little methylated spirit to remove traces of grease. Use as little glue as possible, and while it is drying, keep the corners clamped together with special picture clamps. You can buy these from art shops, ironmongers and Do-It-Yourself shops. They are not expensive and are essential if you are going to do a good job.

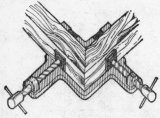

If the frame is heavy you may wish to reinforce the corners. To do this you can buy metal plates which are similar to those used for strengthening weak joints in furniture. They are triangular and come with holes ready drilled in them, so that they can be screwed into the wood. You buy them from Do-It-Yourself shops and hardware stores, together with the right size screws.

4. *Re-finishing*. With the frame clean and mended, it may still need re-finishing. This is described between pages 89 and 99. Good quality wood will only require a wax polish. If the surface is scratched, or if you don't like the finish, it can be sanded down (page 91), waxed and left as natural wood. If the frame is veneered – that is, if a thin layer of good wood has been applied on top of the base wood – and the veneer is loose, it will have to be stuck down again with woodwork adhesive, as described on page 88. If the wood isn't very good or if you are in the mood to experiment, it can be painted (pages 95–96) or gilded. Gilding would be the most appropriate finish for the frame of a 'masterpiece'. A wax or liquid leaf like those made by Winsor & Newton is best; follow the maker's instructions when applying it. An aerosol produces a perfectly acceptable finish but is rather hard to control when you're applying it to such a narrow surface. The process is described more fully on pages 96–99.

Re-mounting

Before the frame can be re-assembled the picture must be re-mounted on a fresh backing. As with all other sticking jobs involving paper, the best materials are the ones used for photographic mounting. They will certainly not grow fungus like the old flour-and-water paste.

The card you use for mounting should be exactly the same size as the frame, no matter what the size of the picture. If the picture is smaller than the frame, and if you are not using a separate card or paper frame to set it off, then choose a suitable colour for the mounting card as this will be seen.

Stick the picture in the centre of the card, leaving a slightly deeper margin at the bottom of the card than at the top. When the picture is mounted draw straight pencil lines round it to give it a neat outline.

Using just a mounting sheet to set off your picture is the least satisfactory method. It can easily look very amateur if your glueing is not perfect, or the edges of the picture are not quite straight. You get a more professional-looking job if you set a card mat between the picture and the glass, with a window cut in the centre to frame the picture.

Take a sheet of card which is a suitable colour and cut it to the same size as the frame. Measure the picture and draw a rectangle of exactly the same dimensions on the card. Make sure it is accurately placed to match the position of the picture on the mounting card. Cut out the rectangle to leave a window through which the picture will show. The cutting can't be done with scissors as you would have to bend the card. Instead you should lay it flat, making sure the surface it rests on is well-protected, and go round it with a sharp Stanley knife. Use a bevel gauge set at an angle of 90° to keep the corner accurate. You can then push the centre out of the card, leaving the mat with the correct-size window in the middle. Draw round the edges in pencil or thin gold lines to neaten it off.

Dealing with the Inner Frame

Lastly, if you are using an inner frame between the glass and the frame itself, make sure this is the size and colour you want. The most common type is made up of four mitred strips of wood. You can buy the length you require from art shops. However, there is no reason why you should not use wider strips if you want to, though you will have to cut and finish them yourself. This is often a good idea when you have a very small picture but want to use a largish frame to prevent its getting lost. Cut four mitred strips of hardboard the length and depth of the frame, using a fret-saw. Then either gild them with wax or liquid leaf (page 98), or cover them in a material such as velvet. If you use fabric cut it a little larger than the wood and stick it with a minimum amount of glue, tucking the excess material under, on to the wrong side. If the existing inner frame is the right size but looks shabby, you can re-gild it if necessary, according to the methods described on pages 96–99.

Re-assembly

With all the component parts cleaned and mended, and the picture mounted on fresh card, you can put the whole package back together again.

Place the frame face-down. Slot the inner frame, if you are using one, right into the rebates, and place the glass on top. If you aren't using an inner frame, slot the glass straight into the rebates.

If the picture is smaller than the frame and you are setting it off with a card frame, put this in, face-down. Next comes the picture mounted on card; be sure to get this as straight and central as possible. If you're using a card frame to set off the picture, the mount itself mustn't show through at all.

If you are using a sheet of card treated with Thymol Solution or a proprietary sterilising mixture to prevent any growth of fungus, this should come next. The card should be treated with Thymol Solution or a proprietary mixture and left until thoroughly dry before being used. The backing board (either the original or a replacement cut to the size of the frame) should be placed on top of all these and the tacks bent down over it. These tacks should be fixed firmly enough to prevent the glass from falling back. If the existing tacks are not sufficient or strong enough, knock in some more at right angles to the inner edge of the frame; 12·5 mm gimp pins are good for this job.

Finally cover your handiwork with a sheet of strong brown paper stuck down with gummed strip. Don't neglect this or the dust will soon get into the frame.

Hanging

To hang the newly-framed picture, screw in a pair of the special screws which are available from art shops and iron-mongers. These have rings on the top for taking the wire or string. Sometimes the wood may be too well-seasoned for the screws to go into the frame and you must then resort to bang-ing in a couple of nails and tying the string to them.

In order to keep a free passage for the air to circulate round the picture, stick a small piece of cork on the back, which will keep it away from the wall.

Cutting a Frame down to Size

Where a frame is too large for the picture you have in mind for it, it can be cut down to size. It usually takes a little practice to get the corners right.

From the top left-hand corner of the frame measure the length of the frame you require along the top side, and the depth of the frame you require down the left-hand side. Cut the frame, using a fret-saw, at an angle of 45°, so that you can make mitred corners. Repeat the process, measuring up and along from the bottom right-hand corner, and cutting the frame at an angle of 45° to match up with its opposite number.

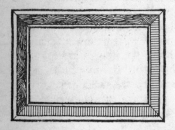
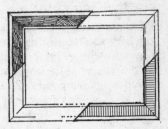

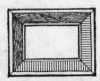

Glue the new corners together, keeping them firmly in position with corner cramps. If you like to nail the wood as well, use corrugated clamps, hammering them in across the joint to draw the wood together.

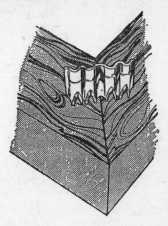

When the glue has dried the corners can be further reinforced with metal plates. You can then get a piece of picture glass cut to fit the new frame.

Framing Needlework

Samplers, tapestries, and so on should be cleaned as described on pages 100–104 and mounted on a canvas or nylon backing. Buy this from an art or needlework shop. Use an inner frame to separate the needlework from the glass. If you want to hang needlework or tapestry unframed, let the backing take the weight by sewing the hooks on to it, not on to the tapestry itself.

Wood

Introduction

The methods of restoring wooden junk described in this chapter are adequate for most straightforward jobs. You can in time progress from the simpler methods of repairing and refinishing described here, to experimenting with different antique finishes or tackling jobs like 'cannibalising' – using the good bits of several pieces of furniture to make one new piece.

One word of warning. Central heating can have a devastating effect on wood. The dry atmosphere causes shrinking and warping, and veneer (the thin layer of 'good' wood sometimes applied to give a nice-looking finish) tends to come loose. You can protect your hard work to some extent if you hide little dishes of water under the furniture to keep the air a bit more humid, or you can buy an electric humidifier.

Trees are divided into two types, hardwoods and softwoods. This is usually an accurate description of the type of timber they produce. However, because the categories are based on botanical differences, such as how the trees seed, there are some rather startling exceptions. Balsa wood, for example, is technically a hardwood in spite of its soft texture.

Softwoods are generally pale or pinkish in colour and they don't have a very distinctive grain. For this reason they are used for carpentry and building work where appearance is not the main consideration, and they're usually painted over.

The best-known softwoods are pine and spruce, which turn up as plywood and whitewood furniture. They are very easy to work with and cheap to buy.

Hardwoods usually come from tropical areas. They tend to have a more beautiful grain than softwoods and a thin layer – a veneer – of hardwood is sometimes used to give an expensive finish to cheaper wood. Untreated hardwoods come in a wide range of colours but the colours we associate with them – the rich shade of mahogany, for example – are the results of traditional stains. These protect the wood and enhance the pattern of the grain.

The best-known hardwoods are walnut, a golden wood with dark streaks, which is a favourite veneer; oak, which is pale brown and contains acid and tannin – this can cause nails to corrode; beech, another pale wood, which is even stronger than oak; mahogany, which comes in two varieties, African and American, and which is usually a reddish colour, and is used for very high quality work.

Here are a few fairly straightforward examples of pieces you might buy to restore:

BOXES: look out for school tuck-boxes, usually made of pine. When stripped down and re-finished, they can look very old and intriguing. Their metal bands and hinges look good when re-lacquered. Small boxes can be restored and used for cigarettes, sweets, playing cards, and so on, and make good presents. You can often pick them up cheaply if the hinge is missing or broken – two problems which are easily dealt with.

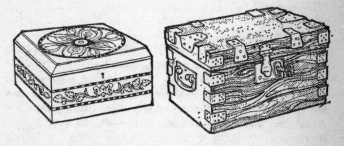

CHAIRS: Victorian kitchen chairs are a good buy. They are common enough to make it possible to collect a set, and they look very good painted. Even modern chairs may have potentially attractive wood hidden under the thick layer of glossy varnish sprayed on at the factory. Wobbly legs can often be cured with metal brackets.

CHESTS OF DRAWERS look good when stripped down and re-painted. Missing handles and knobs can easily be replaced (brass knobs look attractive on a white-painted chest). Stiff drawers may require nothing more drastic than a little polish rubbed into the sides. Drawers which seem a bit too musty for clothes can be sweetened with Mary Chess scented lacquer. A wardrobe could be given a matching coat of paint to make a 'set'.

TABLES: small ones are very common in junk shops, and of course it is usually the surface which is damaged. If the veneer is past repair, you can strip it right off and paint the table instead. Stained french polish can be revived and shaky legs steadied.

HAT STANDS are useful for the very purpose for which they were originally intended, and if you paint them white or a bright colour they won't be too gloomy for a modern house. They are also handy in the bathroom to hang dressing gowns and towels on.

Woodworm

The Worm and its Effects
Woodworm is the larva of a tiny winged beetle which flies from one carefully restored treasure to another laying its eggs. The larvae gorge themselves on the wood, leaving a network of wriggly tunnels behind them. In the summer they turn into beetles themselves and emerge in their turn to lay eggs and repeat the cycle. After a few seasons of woodworm infestation, a piece of wood is transformed into a fragile shell – particularly unfortunate if the piece in question happens to be a chair-leg.

How to Check for Woodworm
A quick way of judging whether the piece of furniture you are considering is currently infested is by looking for piles of fine wood dust and fresh exit holes where the wood looks bright and new. Check for these exit holes in areas which usually escape notice – behind mirrors and pictures, at the back of the wardrobe, under the piano. Often furniture which is solid to

look at and protected by varnish and lacquer, is backed by cheap wood where woodworm has been on the rampage. Country-made grandfather clocks are a good example.

Unfortunately, worm holes aren't always present to indicate that a piece of furniture is infested, if none of the larvae have yet emerged. You can buy something which looks perfect, but woodworm are already lurking inside. So before you commit yourself to buying, tap the piece and look to see if any tell-tale dust falls out. If there are some signs of woodworm in an otherwise attractive piece it is probably still worth buying it, and treating it with an insecticide. Don't let the infected piece near anything else until it has been treated.

How to Treat Woodworm
Once you spot woodworm in any of your furniture isolate it and treat it with an insecticide immediately. Rentokil and Cuprinol make insecticides especially for treating woodworm. They usually come in liquid form, in a tin with a special applicator. The applicator makes it easier to get the liquid right into the wood through the worm holes.

Rentokil also sell a very handy aerosol spray which can be squirted into the worm holes. This simplifies things if you are trying to treat a very large surface.

Always begin by reading the maker's instructions, as you must be careful not to get any of the liquid on your skin or to breathe in the fumes. If possible take the piece you are going to treat into the fresh air, or open all the windows and keep them open for several hours to allow the fumes to escape. Wear an overall or old clothes, and protect your hands with rubber gloves. If you are going to use an aerosol spray put a scarf over your mouth and nose as the spray tends to rebound off the wood. Always repeat the whole process after an interval of about three weeks.

Be extra fastidious in the summer months when woodworm is likely to spread, and keep an eye open for any tell-tale holes or dust.

If the infestation has gone so far that the piece of wood is almost rotten it is best to cut away the damaged wood and replace it. Don't economise by substituting plywood – woodworm is wild about it.

Once you have treated a damaged piece of furniture for woodworm, it is a good idea to fill the holes with a wood filler, such as paraffin wax or plastic wood. Not only does this give you some way of judging whether the infestation has been halted, it also improves the appearance and strengthens the wood. (This is not only done on junk but on good quality antiques.) Squeeze the plastic wood or wax on to the wood, give it a few minutes to get into the holes, apply some more if it sinks in a long way, and sand off the excess when it dries. If more than one layer of plastic wood is needed, wait until the first layer is dry before applying it. This takes about an hour. Sometimes expensive antiques are allowed to look worm-ridden as a supposed proof of their age, but restored junk should look as good as possible.

How to Prevent Woodworm

Unfortunately you can never guarantee to prevent woodworm. Lately a strain has developed with a certain degree of immunity to insecticides. However, you may like to treat wooden pieces with one of the anti-woodworm polishes made by Rentokil or Cuprinol. These serve the same sort of purpose as mothballs, and to be effective they must be applied *everywhere*, especially to hidden areas like the back of a piano or the underside of a table.

All the products for treating woodworm are readily available from Do-It-Yourself shops and ironmongers.

Repairs

When repairing or re-finishing, you will get the best results if you keep the surfaces you are working on free from dirt and grease.

Mending Loose Joints

1. *Glueing.* Glue is perfectly adequate for most simple repairs, unless you are mending something which is in for really hard wear, or something which is going to have to stand up under weight – a chair, for instance.

You can either use adhesive for the complete repair job on a joint, or to reinforce a joint which has been mended with nails and plates. It is also used to repair veneer and marquetry.

Clean the surfaces which are to be glued together (a section about cleaning begins on page 86). Decide which type of glue is best suited to the job you are doing – the paragraphs about Scotch Glue and modern adhesives on pages 78–80 should help; apply a thin layer. It is important to apply the minimum amount of glue consistent with a secure join. Adhesive can be applied to awkward surfaces with a syringe. Join the two pieces together. The glue will be more effective if applied to surfaces which have been slightly warmed and if the job is done in a warm room.

You will need to apply pressure to the join until the glue has dried. This can be done by tying the pieces tightly together, or by weighting or cramping.

Tying is probably the best method on awkward joins, assuming that there won't be a great deal of pressure on the joint when it is mended.

Weighting (with books, or scale weights) is ideal for flat surface repairs, such as glueing leather on to a desk top.

Cramping, however, is the most efficient way of keeping the two surfaces together, and is essential if you want a really secure repair.

You can buy cramps from ironmongers or Do-It-Yourself shops. Practise fixing them to the join *before* you apply the glue: it will be too late to work out the best points of pressure when the adhesive is already half-dry.

When weighting a join, put a protective covering, such as a piece of felt, between the wood and the weight.

When cramping, put a block of wood between the cramp and the surface you are mending, to prevent the cramp from biting into the wood and causing further damage. It is always an advantage to have another person to help you fix the cramps on to a join.

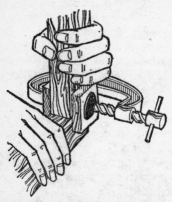

The standard cabinet makers' joints can become loose with age, especially if they have been in an over-dry atmosphere. If this is the case you should take them apart, clean them thoroughly and glue them back together again. Clamp them securely until the glue is dry. If the joins no longer fit perfectly and there are gaps, wedge slices of fresh wood into the spaces. Secure these with adhesive.

SCOTCH GLUE is the original wood adhesive and still readily available from Do-It-Yourself shops, if you want to use authentic materials. It is organic in origin and therefore subject to fungus growths. It has the disadvantage of being water soluble so take care if you are cleaning any furniture with soap and water; the joints may come apart or the veneer suddenly lift off. Scotch Glue can't be used on top of a previous application: all the traces of the old glue must be completely cleaned off. Because of these disadvantages, and because it has to be mixed, it has been largely replaced by stronger, less temperamental modern adhesives, but it is still the favourite adhesive for veneering and many craftsmen still prefer to use it.

You can either buy Scotch Glue as a powder or in resinous lumps. To make it up you will need a double saucepan; or, if you like, you can buy a special glue pot when you get the glue. You can also improvise by standing a pan in a saucepan or tray. Measure out the recommended quantity into the inner pot, breaking any lumps up into small pieces. Cover this with water and leave to soak overnight. Then fill the outer pan half-full of water.

Put the glue pot over a gentle heat, and let the glue in the inner pan melt slowly. If it is too thick add a little more water; if it is too thin add a little more glue. Aim to get the glue to a treacly consistency, and use it while it is still hot.

Another glue used by craftsmen and cabinet makers rather than Do-It-Yourself enthusiasts, is CASCAMITE. Like Scotch Glue it has the disadvantage that it has to be mixed, but unlike Scotch Glue it is waterproof.

MODERN WOODWORKERS' ADHESIVES, such as the one made by Evostick, are generally good if the maker's instructions are followed properly, and sufficient pressure is applied to the join for a sufficient length of time. Contact (or impact) adhesives are not really suitable for wood.

The most powerful all-purpose adhesive is an epoxy resin such as Araldite or Dunlop epoxy adhesive. When you buy it you get two tubes; one contains the glue itself, the other the hardener. When you are ready to glue something, you combine equal quantities from each tube, mixing them on a small piece of glass, using the spatula in the packet. (Don't worry too much if you don't have a suitable piece of glass, I've seen good results obtained after mixing the two components on a piece of cardboard.) Once the adhesive has hardened it's almost impossible to shift, so you must know exactly what you intend to do before you start, and not mix too much at a time. It's difficult to get off your skin as well, and can make you feel quite itchy. It is best to wear thin polythene surgical gloves from the chemist's or drugstore, which protect you without making you clumsy. If you get any adhesive on your skin, wash it off immediately. Methylated spirit will remove epoxy adhesives if used before they harden.

2. *Nailing*. As you will find when you first go to buy them, nails come in a bewildering array of shapes and sizes. Apart from corrugated fasteners (mentioned in the framing chapter) and the multi-purpose gimp pins and tacks, you're going to need round wire nails, and lost-head nails.

THE ROUND WIRE NAIL is the traditionally shaped nail which is suitable for most jobs and which is easy to use. It does, however, have the disadvantage that the head shows, being raised slightly above the surface of the wood, and so is best used in places where it will be hidden, such as the underside of a chair.

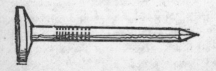

THE LOST-HEAD NAIL is exactly what it says: a nail which has virtually no head. This type of nail can be knocked below the surface of the wood with a nail punch, and then hidden by the application of a little plastic wood. Plastic wood will take any finish you choose and the nailing will be invisible. If you find a nailed joint which needs mending, remove the original nails with pliers or the claw end of a small hammer. With your small hammer, you should then knock in new nails. You can't use the same nail holes, for the wood will be weakened or damaged, but you should follow the *angle* of the original nails. You'll probably also want to strengthen the joint with adhesive.

3. *Dowelling*. Another method of mending is dowelling. You may either want to remove and replace old broken dowels in a dowelled joint, or you may decide dowelling would be a better method than glueing or nailing if you are trying to mend an ordinary break.

Dowels are wooden pins which fit into ready-drilled holes, as shown overleaf. You can buy them in packets at your local Do-It-Yourself shop. You can usually get the right diameter without any trouble (6 mm diameter is very common), but you may have to cut them to the right length yourself.

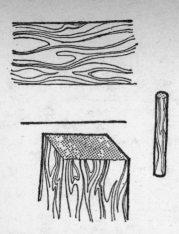

Drill two holes, of equal length and the right diameter, one on each side of the join. The dowel should go at right angles to the break or the joint. (Make sure that you use the right size bit in your drill.) If you are mending a broken joint, you may need to drill away the original dowel. Always make sure the wood is free of dirt and old glue.

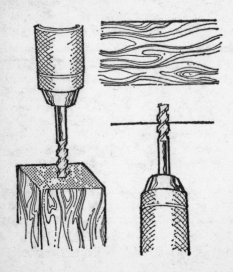

Drip a little glue into one hole and then fit in the dowel pin. It should fit snugly but not so tightly that it has to be forced into the hole. When the pin is secure, slot it into the other hole. You may like to use a little glue at the join as well as in the dowel hole. In some cases you may be able to drill the dowel hole in one operation, through both pieces of wood, and glue the dowel into place in a single operation as well.

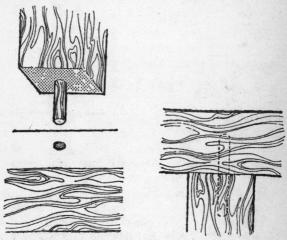

4. *Metal brackets*. If dowelling is beyond you, or if the joint is a concealed one and you don't want to waste a lot of effort on it, metal brackets and plates are a good idea. If the joint is going to take a lot of strain, then it is worth adding metal brackets anyway, for extra strength. They are very useful for repairing wobbly chair legs and table legs.

Basically, metal brackets are right angles of steel which brace the joint and take the strain. You can buy them in a wide variety of sizes at a Do-It-Yourself shop. The salesman will advise you on the best kind to buy for the job you have in mind. He will also make sure you buy the right size screws. The brackets have holes in them already to take the screws.

This type of repair is easier if you glue the joint together first and then use the bracket for extra strength. Hold the bracket in position and use a pencil to mark the position of the screw-holes. Then, using a bit a fraction of a size smaller than the screws, drill a hole in the wood to give the screws a start before screwing the bracket into place with a screwdriver. The metal can then be painted over so that it merges with the wood.

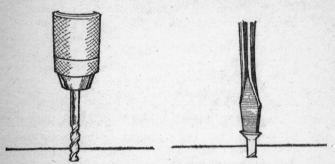

Screws

There are one or two points worth mentioning about using screws. When fitting screws into wood you should drill a hole about half the length of the screw to give it a start. This hole should be no larger in diameter than the shank of the screw itself. If it is too wide the thread of the screw will have nothing to bite into and will slip out. If in doubt use a bit slightly smaller than the diameter of the shank of the screw. The wider part at the top of the screw has no thread at all so you will sometimes find it necessary to drill a small space to accommodate it, near the surface of the wood.

A little wax on the shank of the screw will make it easier to drive in and will prevent its going rusty.

When you are replacing old screws you may find it rather difficult to remove the original screws with a screwdriver because the thread has broken. If this is the case, first remove all paint and varnish round the top of the screw and brush a little paraffin round the head. Give it time to soak in and lubricate the area, then use the screwdriver again. If the screw is still obstinate, try applying the tip of a hot poker to the head, taking care not to scorch the surrounding area. The heat from the poker will expand the metal which will enlarge the hole.

Then when the metal has cooled it should be easier to get it out of the enlarged hole.

You can sometimes loosen a screw by placing a screwdriver in the head and giving it a sharp tap with a hammer.

Replacing Hinges and Handles
Unbroken hinges and handles may be useless because the wood into which they are screwed is damaged, and the screws are loose in their holes. The obvious thing to do is to give them a new secure base. If the wood is damaged and splitting badly, cut away the whole area and glue in a replacement section, as shown in the illustration, to which you can then screw the hinge or handle. Don't worry too much about whether the new wood matches the original, for most of it will be concealed by the metal. If you think any of the new wood will show, stain or polish it to as near a match as you can get, or see if you can take a matching piece of wood from an article beyond repair. (If you are going to be doing a lot of this work it is useful to keep a small selection ready.)

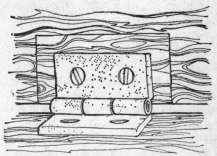

If the surrounding wood is sound but the screw holes seem to have become enlarged, plug the screw holes with new wood as if you were putting in a dowel, making sure, however, that the top of the plug is flush with the surface. (Dowelling pins would probably be the best thing to use.)

When you're replacing the hinge or handle, use new screws as the thread on the old ones will probably be broken. Don't forget to give the screws a start by drilling a small hole as just described.

If the hinge or handle itself is broken you may be able to find a good replacement on a piece of junk past repair. Again it is worth keeping any you find for future use. Alternatively, you can buy a new one from a handicraft shop (these tend to stock modern designs), or from a shop like Beardmores (see page 41). They have a mail order catalogue with a wide range of designs and also make special period designs for items such as writing boxes.

Cleaning and Restoring Existing Wood Finishes

It isn't always necessary to do a complete re-finishing job on a junk item; a good clean and re-waxing may be adequate. In fact you should always think twice with any reasonably good piece before removing all the evidence and patina of age. Even with something quite ordinary there's no point in doing more work than is absolutely necessary. Begin by cleaning.

Cleaning
Grease can be removed by wiping the surface of the wood with a cloth wrung out in methylated spirit – but *don't* use methylated spirit on a varnished or french polished surface as this will dissolve the finish. To remove wax, use a cloth wrung out in turpentine or turpentine substitute (white spirit). Dirty wood can be washed with soap and water – don't, however, slop water about liberally as it may damage glued joints (Scotch Glue is soluble in water) and may even cause the wood to swell. Stains, such as ink stains, can be removed with a weak solution of a domestic bleach – Domestos, for instance.

Reviving French Polish
French polish is the hard glossy finish usually found on grand pianos and similar furniture. Although it seems a very resilient finish, it's easily damaged, particularly by heat. The heat draws up moisture from the wood underneath and this produces a filmy effect in the polish. By applying hot dusters to the mark you can sometimes release this moisture.

Stained and dull french polish can be 'revived'. There are several home recipes for doing this and also proprietary brands of 'reviver' on the market. This is the one I use myself:

> one part vinegar;
> one part methylated spirit;
> one part real turpentine.

Mix them together and then add one part linseed oil. Make up about ¼ litre (1¼ cupfuls) to begin with, and apply it on a soft pad, using a circular motion.

Scratches
If there are only a few scratches on an otherwise acceptable finish, they can be treated with a proprietary scratch camouflage, such as Joy Scratch Dressing. This comes in two shades, for light and dark wood. It is applied to the scratch marks with a soft brush.

Removing and Replacing Damaged Veneer
Veneer is the term used for a thin facing of good decorative wood, like walnut or mahogany, which is stuck to a base of cheaper wood. When the veneer is made up of a pattern composed of small pieces of several types of wood this is called marquetry.

Originally veneer was stuck down with Scotch Glue. This is still used, although some people prefer to use a modern PVA adhesive. Because Scotch Glue is water soluble, it's easy to remove any damaged veneer by steaming it off, using a warm iron over a damp cloth.

Before you decide to remove a piece of veneer, however, make sure it is really damaged. If the veneer has simply lifted a little (which it will do if the atmosphere is too dry) you can easily stick it down again. Raise the loose veneer gently as far as it will go and remove the old glue with a little warm water. When the bare wood is clean and dry pour a thin layer of warm Scotch Glue or a water-soluble adhesive under the veneer. Press the veneer down and wipe away any excess glue which oozes out. Weight the veneer until the glue dries, remembering to put a layer of felt between the veneer and the weight to protect the surface.

Repairing veneer which is actually damaged is finicky rather than difficult, but you will need to invest in a fret-saw to cut out replacement shapes. Handicraft shops sell strips of thin wood which you can stain to an approximate colour, but this is not really very satisfactory. It's far better to get hold of the right sort of wood, and it's a good idea to keep a box full of old bits of veneer which you can match up; a box of old spare nails is also useful.

Cut out the damaged section, taking care to make an easy shape such as a square, and trace its outline on tracing paper. With Sellotape, stick the tracing paper over the piece of veneer you are going to use for the repair, placing it along the same grain as the original. Now cut round this paper pattern with a fret-saw. Be over-generous rather than niggardly: it is much better to sand off any excess than to risk cutting a patch which is too small.

Stick the new veneer into place (making sure the base wood is clean and grease-free), using Scotch Glue or a modern, preferably water-soluble, adhesive. Be sparing with the adhesive as any excess will seep through the veneer and may stain.

Place a protective layer, such as a piece of felt, over the veneer and weight it with a heavy book. Don't take the pressure off the join until the glue is quite dry – about forty-eight hours, *but longer if possible.*

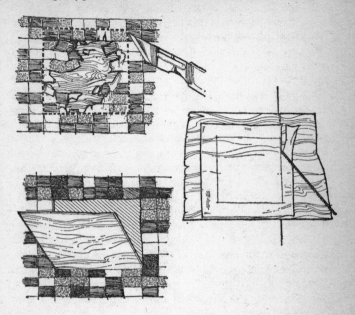

Re-finishing

If the finish is really bad it will have to be done afresh. There are several possibilities open to you. Whichever one you decide on, you can be certain that the whole process will take longer than you expected. It is best to work on a small area at a time so that you are spurred on by seeing results and comparing them with the unfinished areas. However, when it comes to the final staining or painting you should do the whole thing in one fell swoop or it won't match.

Another thing you can be pretty sure of is that you are going to make a lot of dust and dirt, so be prepared with plenty of newspaper on the floor, and wear protective clothing. When removing an old surface wear a scarf over your nose and mouth to keep the dust out.

Removing Old Paint and Varnish with a Paint Stripper

If an item is painted or varnished you will have to begin by removing the whole finish. There are several proprietary brands of remover and/or thinner for paints and varnishes, and there's not much to choose between them. Begin by reading the maker's instructions – and do wear gloves as even a small drop of paint stripper can give you a nasty burning sensation.

Paint the remover on to the surface and leave it for about ten minutes (the time may vary with the make; the instructions will tell you), and then scrape it off with a sharp paint scraper.

This is better than trying to wipe it off with a cloth which will do nothing but smear the varnish around and rub it into the wood. However, don't expect a really clean surface after using a paint stripper as some of the stain may have soaked below the surface of the wood. Be very careful when using the scraper; don't apply so much pressure that you score the wood, for deep scratches are difficult to erase completely. Often good results are obtained by using medium grade (oo) steel wool in conjunction with the paint stripper. This is the best method for delicate furniture or a french polished surface.

When the paint or lacquer has been stripped off you will need to smooth the surface by sanding with glass paper or steel wool.

Sanding

This process may either be carried out to complete the work begun with a paint stripper, or as a first stage in itself. You can either use a mechanical sander or sand by hand. Since all the methods in this book are for people who want to keep costs to a minimum, I'm not suggesting you should go straight out and buy a power drill and all its attachments just to do one small job. It will, however, save you a lot of time and effort if you have access to a power sander, especially one with the most valuable attachment of all – a willing friend to show you how it works.

Mechanical sanders have a circular movement, and if used carelessly can leave circular grooves in the wood which are almost impossible to remove. Because they work very fast, disasters like this can overtake you before you are aware what is happening. Only use power sanders on flat surfaces – they will flatten curved surfaces, such as chair legs. Don't use them for delicate work.

Taking off an entire surface by sanding by hand can be exhausting, so do it in stages. You will need glass paper or steel wool, which is available from handicraft shops.

Glass paper is exactly what it says – crushed glass on backing paper. It's sometimes called sand paper because originally sanding was done with coarse sand mounted on backing paper.

Glass paper and steel wool are available in different grades, and with practice you will become more choosy about which grade to use for which job. Glass paper is often sold in packs of assorted grades. Grade f2 glass paper or grade o steel wool are adequate for most purposes.

Don't try sanding by wrapping the glass paper round your index finger; you will only succeed in making a narrow groove in the wood. It is much simpler to wrap the glass paper round a flat block of wood, which increases the area you can cover with a single stroke. You can buy a block for this purpose from a handicraft shop or you can make do with the back of a scrubbing brush. Don't rub constantly over the edges of a flat surface or you will round them off. Apply pressure as evenly as possible and work along the grain of the wood. If you go against the grain this will show through when you come to finish the surface with paint or varnish.

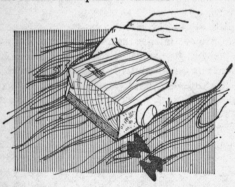

Deciding on a New Finish
When you've acquired as smooth a surface as possible, you can decide which finish to apply. The type of finish depends largely on the state of the wood itself. Don't forget that the finish is

not simply to beautify the wood, but is a protection against dirt and damp, so bear in mind the type of life the piece is going to lead.

Natural Finishes

If the wood has an attractive grain and isn't disfigured by scratches and dents, you'll probably like to leave it looking natural. You can apply shellac or oil the wood with linseed oil to seal and darken it; an oiled finish tends to look matt even when waxed. Apply the oil or shellac carefully with a good quality brush as it darkens the wood which easily becomes streaky. For a specific colour use a coloured woodstain (see below).

When the oil or shellac is dry and the colour is as deep as you want it, sand the surface lightly with steel wool. Then polish it with beeswax polish. It will take several applications to build up a good shine, but it's worth the effort. A power drill with a polishing accessory is a great time-saver. Don't use polishes which contain silicones (check the list of ingredients on the tin) as these tend to seal in the dirt. The standard recipe for making beeswax polish is as follows:

Put a watertight container, such as an old biscuit tin, into a bowl of boiling water. Half-fill the tin with best quality beeswax, which you can buy from the chemist's or drugstore. When this has melted add an equal quantity of pure turpentine. Remove the tin from the hot water and mix the two ingredients thoroughly together while they are still liquid. (Keep the lid on the tin when the polish isn't in use or it will dry up.)

The Use of Fillers, Stains and Sealers

The colours we associate with various woods – oak, mahogany, walnut – are to a great extent the results of the traditional stains used by furniture makers in the past. You can go a long way towards achieving an authentic finish by following the same methods. Before you apply a stain, however, decide whether or not you will also need a filler and/or sealer.

1. *Fillers.* All the best-known woods, except pine, benefit from the use of a filler before the finish is applied. This is

because they have large pores which will otherwise absorb the stain unevenly and leave a blotchy, unprofessional finish. The time involved in using a filler is minimal and more than justified by the improved results.

Buy Brummer, a semi-transparent paste filler, from handicraft shops or ironmongers'. Thin it with turpentine until it is a creamy consistency, and apply it with a brush. Plastic wood also makes an excellent filler for large imperfections and takes a stain very well. Apply the filler according to the maker's instructions and when it's dry sand the surface down.

As filler contains water it will shrink slightly when dry so be generous when applying it.

2. *Staining*. The most authentic stain that you can use is an aniline dye. It comes as a powder which is dissolved in water. To achieve the shade you want, add the powder by degrees, dissolving each addition thoroughly before putting in more. The dye is obtainable in a variety of colours from good handicraft shops or leather shops.

Don't slosh it on too liberally or you may loosen glued joints. If it causes the wood to swell a little, you can easily sand it down when the surface has dried.

A simpler but very good alternative is a wood stain like Rustins which can be applied straight from the tin.

Alternatively you can use one of the polyurethane stains described under point 4, in which case you can skip the sealer stage altogether. When using a non-polyurethane stain, however, you next apply a sealer.

3. *Sealers*. A sealer of varnish is usually applied on top of the stain. This gives added protection against dirt and moisture. The extra expense and effort is particularly worthwhile for practical furniture like tables and chairs.

Buy the wood sealer from handicraft shops or the ironmonger's. If it contains polyurethane this will prevent you from building up a really rich patina with polish. Nevertheless most people nowadays use a clear polyurethane varnish.

When the stain (and sealer if used) has dried, polish the surface with a beeswax polish, as already described on page 93.

4. *Polyurethane stains*. Polyurethane stains are modern plastic stains which seal and stain all in one, and give a

very durable finish. When dried they can be painted over with a matching varnish so that you can have a shiny or matt finish as you choose. They are sold in hardware and handicraft shops and are available in colours labelled 'Oak', 'Mahogany', and so on. These names should only be taken as a rough guide, as you can't make plywood look like mahogany just by using a polyurethane stain. They are quick and easy but won't respond to wax polishing with the rich glow you get from more traditional methods of finishing. Another disadvantage is that the colour builds up with each application. It is therefore always better to start with a much lighter shade than the one you think you want.

Painting

Paint is the obvious answer when the wood isn't particularly beautiful in its own right. Avoid the temptation to slap on a single top coat and let it go at that. Apply the paint in a north/south as well as an east/west direction.

Painting should be done in three stages:

1. *Priming:* use a special wood primer from handicraft shops. Woolworth sells an excellent primer/sealer called Cover-Plus. For very absorbent finishes thin it down with white spirit. Apply the primer with a brush or paint roller. It's possible to dispense with this stage, but the resulting surface may not be as smooth.

2. *Filling:* fill dents and holes with plastic wood or Brummer, to obtain a smooth surface. Simply paste the filler over the holes using a paint scraper or a knife, and wait until it is dry. Sand down any excess. Special knotting can be bought to cover unsightly knot holes.

Of course if the wood is in good condition without any knot holes and dents this stage will not be necessary.

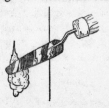

3. *Apply two separate undercoats*, sanding each one lightly when it has dried (this won't, of course, be necessary if you're using a paint which states specifically that it does not need an undercoat) and *one thin top coat* of gloss or emulsion paint – depending on the type of finish you're looking for and the amount of wear the piece will take. Gloss is probably better for chairs and tables. (Use paint stripper to clean emulsion paint off your brushes, white spirit to clean off gloss paint.)

French Polishing
The simplest way of doing your own french polishing is to use a ready-made-up polish. Joy or Rustins are good and come in different shades, for use on light or dark woods.

Tiling
Re-surfacing a table-top with ceramic tiles can produce an unusual and attractive piece of furniture, which is resistant to heat and stains. This can be done with tiles from old fireplaces or you can buy very attractive modern tiles in hardware stores. A good alternative would be the mirror tiles usually sold to be used in bathrooms. They can be stuck on with cement from the Polyfilla range, or you can buy special waterproof grouting.

Gilding
Real gilding is very expensive as it is done with thin sheets of pure gold. It's also very difficult to get a good finish. If you have bought something with real gilding which needs renovation you may prefer to take it to an expert. However, in case you're really keen to try, the method for water gilding is given, which is the most useful for an amateur as it can be used on items like furniture or picture frames. There are also some very cheap and effective alternatives, which are described in the last section of this chapter.

All the products mentioned in the following paragraphs are obtainable from art shops.

Water Gilding
Cover the wood evenly with a good coating of gesso (this is a mixture of whiting and size which can be bought ready made-

up at a good art shop) and leave this to harden. If there is any moulding or other ornamentation, you will have to carve round it when the gesso has dried.

Next the gesso is coated with gold size and left until it is almost, but not quite, dry. At this stage the gold leaf should be pressed on to the size, one leaf at a time. (You buy the gold leaf in books of almost translucent leaves. There are several types and shades to choose from.) The leaves should all point in the same direction and they should overlap very slightly so that there are no gaps.

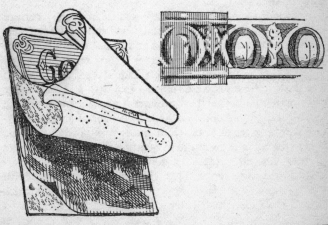

When the object is completely covered it should be smoothed down with a cotton cloth so that none of the joins show and the surface is perfectly smooth.

If you want a glossy finish the gilding should be polished with a burnish made of agate or bloodstone.

Imitation Gilding

Alternatives to real gold leaf give an authentic-looking finish at a fraction of the cost. They can be used on wood or metal or plastic. The liquid kinds can be used as a good substitute for the gold rim so often painted round the edge of bone china.

1. *Spray lacquers* come in a wide variety of metal colours, not just gold but aluminium, copper, silver and most recently brass. Follow the instructions on the can, making sure the surface you're treating is clean, dry and free from grease. Sprays are best for treating large surfaces. When using them mask off adjacent surfaces with special masking Sellotape, so that the edges are clean and straight.

There is an excellent range of colours and finishes called U-spray.

2. *Lacquer*, which comes in small tins, is probably the oldest alternative to real gold leaf and it is easy to apply with a small brush. It's quite cheap, but it has the disadvantage that it too tends to look rather harsh, and it comes in a limited range of shades.

3. *Liquid Leaf.* A better quality lacquer in effect, Treasure Liquid Leaf is suitable for all metal, wood and plastic surfaces. However, the makers recommend you to seal a porous surface with shellac before using it. There is a good range of colours.

4. *Wax.* The firm that markets Liquid Leaf also makes a wax paste. (Reeves make a similar paste with a smaller range of colours.) This is the best product if you want to avoid the harsh effects of the other methods. It is rubbed on to the surface with a finger or a soft cloth and is very satisfying to use. Where the piece of furniture in question is going to be subject to wear and tear, protect the gilding with clear varnish marketed in the same range. This will also give it a glossy finish and is essential for a silver look. If you're not going to varnish it, buff it to a good shine with a soft cloth.

There are a couple of things to note about Treasure Wax and Treasure Liquid Leaf. Firstly, they are both dangerous if taken internally, and if by chance any is swallowed you should get a doctor at once. Don't keep them where a child could get hold of them. Obviously these products should not be used on everyday objects a child might handle, lick or put in its mouth.

Secondly, they can be removed with turpentine if you don't like the effect – and when you want to get the wax off your fingers. This means that if you want to seal them, you shouldn't use a varnish or lacquer which contains turpentine or turpentine substitute (white spirit), as this will dissolve them. But you *can* use turpentine to thin the wax, or to moisten it if it has been in store for a while.

Fabrics and Upholstery

Introduction

Most of the junk fabric you deal with will be upholstery, and it will probably be so worn that you'll be more interested in replacing it than restoring it.

Modern products like Copydex adhesive and washable velvet make the job of re-upholstering and re-covering simpler and longer-lasting.

Once you know the basic technique, you can look with interest at chairs with good frames but appalling tatty covers which are going cheap just because they look so intimidating.

If you get really interested you can go to classes and learn the refinements of upholstering – how to do button backs, for instance.

Upholstery can also transform other furniture. An old box can be converted into a blanket-box-cum-stool by tacking in a lining and covering the lid with a bright material over simple padding. A cutlery canteen makes a good jewellery box if it is re-lined with silk and the lining padded with a little cotton wool. This is described in a little more detail on page 113. Projects like this don't even have the problems associated with re-springing.

You can still find Victorian pin cushions and work bags which are attractive, yet practical. These only need cleaning and perhaps some re-beading, which is simple enough to do if you're interested in needlework. Old-fashioned clothes are popular at present, and among the most versatile are lovely hand-embroidered shawls which you can buy on second-hand clothes stalls and in the large second-hand supermarkets in London.

One out-moded but extremely comfortable piece of furniture is the footstool. This usually has an embroidered or tapestry cover which can be cleaned and repaired without too much trouble.

Cleaning

Washing

While modern detergents and cleaners are excellent for china and glass, they are not to be recommended for old textiles. There *are* exceptions but generally old material is not colourfast and strong detergents cause the dyes to run. In addition the fabric is often very weak and will tend to disintegrate if you apply strong measures. The safest modern product is a Teepol-based one like Stergene, which doesn't leave a scum. Otherwise use pure soap and lukewarm water.

Always make sure that chemicals and soap are rinsed out completely. Wherever possible use distilled water or rain water.

Whites and Lace

You will have to decide how strong you think the material is. If it is fairly sturdy it can be treated with a very mild bleach to get rid of the yellowish tinge which is the almost inevitable result of ageing. If the material seems reasonably strong you can wash it in Stergene and rub it gently to get rid of stubborn dirt. Failing this the pieces should simply be swished around in warm water and Stergene. If you can do this in a really large bowl, you will get more efficient results. Dry flat, and if you are dealing with lace be sure to ease it gently into shape while it is still wet. Really fragile lace should be dry cleaned with fuller's earth.

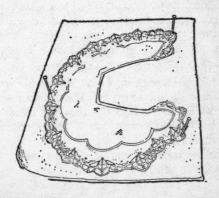

Coloureds

Coloured fabrics should always be tested for colour-fastness on a hidden corner before you go any further. You can safely assume that anything really old will be dyed with vegetable dyes and will *not* be colour-fast. If you feel that the nature of the dirt – especially if the material is a bit smelly – means the fabric needs a wash, then use Stergene in *cold* water. Swish the material round gently, but don't rub or you will start the dye running. Dry the material flat. Never hang it out in direct sunlight, especially if it is wet.

Dry Cleaning

Dry methods should be used on fabric wherever possible as they cut out the possibility of colours running and material drying out of shape. An early dry cleaning method which is very successful on old fabric, especially elaborate pieces like lace, embroidery and needlework, is THE FULLER'S EARTH METHOD. This method is also good for grease-stained leather and for carpeting.

Fuller's earth, which is available from the chemist's or drugstore, should be sprinkled thickly on to the fabric, left for an hour or so to soak up the dirt and grease, and then brushed off with a soft brush (or vacuumed, if you are cleaning a carpet). This can be repeated several times until the fabric is clean, or until the method is no longer being effective. You can try this method using TALCUM POWDER instead of fuller's earth.

GODDARDS DRY CLEAN is a spray which should be applied according to the maker's instructions and left to dry. When the dried powdery residue is brushed away, the dirt and grease go with it.

The same principle applies to the method for cleaning furs. The paler furs should have MAGNESIA POWDER, from the chemist's, rubbed into them. Leave this in for several days while it absorbs the dirt, then take the fur out into the fresh air and brush it thoroughly. For dark fur follow the same method using BRAN, from the pet shop or gardening store, warmed in the oven.

Velvet can be cleaned of fluff and dirt by brushing it lightly with METHYLATED SPIRIT.

CHEMICAL CLEANERS are another method of dry cleaning. If you know of a reliable specialist dry cleaner it may be a good idea to entrust your fabric to him, having explained what the particular problem is. Otherwise you can try the following remedies for the most common stains. When using these methods, always test them on a small patch first as the chemicals could affect the colours. When a grease solvent like carbon tetrachloride or methylated spirit is required, try a proprietary product like Thawpit or Dabitoff.

When you are using chemicals place a wad of material under the fabric you are working on. This will absorb excess liquid and help prevent a mark spreading.

Before trying any of these methods, first try wiping the mark with a cloth wrung out in warm water.

Common Stains

1. *Blood:* if the fabric is colour-fast, soak it overnight in cold, salty water. If this fails or if the fabric is not suitable for wet cleaning, mix a stiff paste of starch with cold water and apply it to the stain. When the paste has dried out brush it off carefully.

2. *Dye:* if the dye runs you may be able to clean it up by sponging the stain with methylated spirit, to which you should add a few drops of ammonia. The chemical should then be rinsed out by sponging with distilled water.

3. *Glue* may be present on upholstery. Dissolve it with a proprietary solvent or acetone (nail-polish remover).

4. *Grease stains and oil stains* should respond to a grease solvent. Try carbon tetrachloride, turpentine substitute (white spirit), methylated spirit or the proprietary brands. Goddards Dry Clean is very effective and does not cause a nasty ring.

5. *Inks:* if the fabric is old you are most likely to be dealing with fountain pen ink. On white fabrics this can be bleached out with a gentle bleach like Milton, or you can create a home-made bleach by sprinkling the stain with salt, rubbing with a cut lemon and leaving for an hour or so before rinsing or sponging off.

On coloured fabrics, sponge the stain first with methylated spirit diluted with an equal quantity of water, then with warm soapy water; then rinse or sponge with clean water. Glycerine will help loosen any particularly stubborn ink stains.

Ball-point ink should be treated with neat methylated spirit and warm suds. Rinse with a damp cloth. Oil of eucalyptus is sometimes successful.

W. H. Smith sells products for removing stains from felt-tip and ball-point pens.

6. *Mildew* is almost impossible to remove. If the material is white, try bleaching. Methylated spirit may also have some effect. Even if you can't remove the stain, you can get rid of the musty smell by washing and/or airing.

7. *Rust and iron mould* is common on upholstery or any material which has been in contact with nails and tacks. Sprinkle salt on the stain and rub with a cut lemon. If this has no effect you can try a rust remover (Boots make one called Movol). A rust remover shouldn't be used on delicate fabrics.

8. *Wax:* scrape off the excess with a knife. Place the fabric on a sheet of clean white blotting paper and hold a hot iron *above* the wax without letting it touch the stain. The melted wax will be soaked up by the blotting paper. Afterwards wash the material according to the methods I've already described, or dry clean.

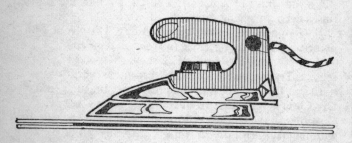

9. *Wine stains:* white fabrics can be bleached with an ordinary domestic bleach like Milton or hydrogen peroxide; colour-fast fabrics can be soaked in a Stergene solution, to which you should add a level tablespoonful of borax for every half-litre (or two cupfuls) of water; non-colour-fast fabrics can be

sponged with a pad wrung out in the same solution. A specialist dry cleaner may also be able to help.

Checking Moth

This is really a matter of prevention rather than cure. The creatures which cause the trouble are the moth larvae. The best way of preventing the larvae is to prevent the moth laying its eggs. Keep susceptible items in a closed cupboard with old-fashioned naphthalene mothballs. Regular airing and shaking out will also help. Mending the small holes is almost impossible although fabrics like tapestry and wool can sometimes be darned.

Upholstery

Old furniture often needs to be re-upholstered. Unsprung furniture is very simple to re-cover. Even when the furniture is sprung, upholstering is not difficult but only a matter of common sense. Basically, you take the original upholstery apart and note carefully the order of the webbing, springs, etc. Then you put the whole thing back together again, replacing any broken components with new ones.

While the upholstery is stripped off, mend or stain the frame, if necessary, according to the methods described in the chapter on wood; and take advantage of the situation to search for any signs of woodworm.

Sprung Upholstery

The first step is taking the original upholstery apart. It is a good idea to keep this job for a fine day and do it out of doors. Alternatively, work in a large room with plenty of newspaper on the floor. To remove the tacks you will need a cabriole hammer, like the one described on page 11. Where tacks and nails are well bedded in, be prepared to resort to improvisation with leverage and brute force. Work from the underneath and towards the cover.

Since each job is very slightly different, it is a good idea when you first start to make a note of what you find – and even a quick sketch. All replacements can be bought at an upholsterer's or a good ironmonger's. You will find that a chair is put together like this:

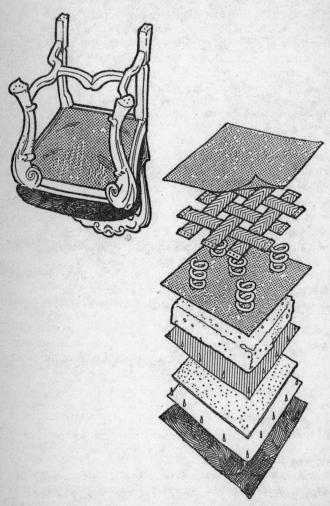

1. *A hessian cover*, to keep out the dirt and hide the tacks;

2. *Webbing* – either flax or, if the chair is fairly modern, rubber; flax webbing will have to be replaced as it will have lost its stretch (if you replace the webbing you may find it unnecessary to buy new springs as well, for often springs only seem to sag because the webbing is over-stretched);

3. *Springs*, which are sewn on to the webbing where the straps cross one another, usually in a pattern of four with one in the middle; you may be able to use the existing springs again, but they must be replaced if they are damaged; and if you decide to replace one spring you must replace them all or you will get a different level of bounce from the new one;

4. *A calico or hessian cover* sewn on to the top of the springs and tacked down to the chair frame; you may prefer to cut a fresh one;

5. *Stuffing* – either kapok, horsehair or latex foam; this can generally be used again when it has been aired and fluffed up afresh, but do check it for clothes moth and other bugs; you can buy new stuffing from the upholsterer's or the haberdashery department – latex foam is quite good but tends to flatten, and most professionals use kapok;

6. *A layer of material* to cover the stuffing, which is tacked down to the frame;

7. *Wadding* (flock) – a thin layer of very soft stuffing to make the chair comfortable and give the seat a good shape;

8. *A calico cover* over the wadding, tacked down to the frame;

9. *A decorative cover;* use this as a pattern for your new cover, and also for the calico cover immediately beneath it. There is usually a *decorative braid* round the edge of the cover to hide the tacks and neaten the work.

Re-upholstering

When you have taken the original upholstery apart, cleaned the frame thoroughly, and replaced any worn parts, you will have to put the whole thing back together again and tack the webbing and covers in place. The tacks should be about $2\frac{1}{4}$ cm apart. It takes a fair amount of practice before you become adept at pulling the calico covers and the decorative cover into shape. It is best to tack down the front and back edges first, and make adjustments by working in the material along the sides.

Do it in the following order.

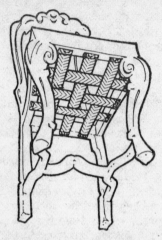

1. *Webbing:* this will have to be stretched round the frame with a webbing stretcher from the upholstery shop, in order to achieve the right tension. Turn the chair over and fix the webbing underneath the frame, or the upholstery will sit too high on the frame.

Cut the strips of webbing about 15 cm longer than the width or length of the frame they will cover. On average you will need three webs each way.

Take your first strip of webbing. Fold under about 2½ cm and tack to one side of the frame with three tacks. Stretch the webbing across to the other side of the frame, and using the stretcher, pull it taut. Tack it into position, cut it off with 2½ cm to spare, fold over the end and fix with an extra tack or two. Repeat this until you have a base of interlaced webbing. The firmer the webbing, the harder the seat.

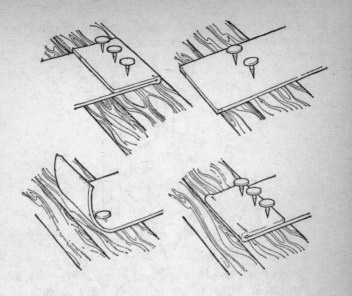

2. *Springs:* you should sew these down to the webbing where it interlaces, using upholsterer's twine.

Concentrate the springs towards the front of the chair. That is where most people sit, and is the area which takes most of the strain.

3. *A calico cover:* place this over the springs and tack it to the frame. Sew the top of the springs to the cover with a few stitches.

4. *Stuffing:* this should be arranged on top of the cover, so that it is highest in the middle and slightly overhanging the sides. Keep it in position by tacking large loops of upholsterer's twine round the edge of the chair and working the stuffing through them, as shown in the illustration.

2a–4a. *Foam:* a cube of latex foam cut to size by a foam converter can be used in place of the springs and stuffing. though this isn't quite as comfortable to sit on. The foam should be flush with the inside of the frame.

5. Cover the stuffing or foam with *a piece of calico* tacked to the frame.
6. *Wadding:* arrange this on top of the calico, using large guide loops as described in point 4.
7. Tack down *a final calico cover.*
8. *A decorative cover:* when choosing this, don't only consider how it will fit into the room's colour scheme, but also

whether it will lead a hectic life and need to be durable. Unless you have much experience of upholstering, it's unwise to choose striped or distinctly patterned materials, or velvet, as you will have difficulty with the nap. It's worth remembering that velvets collect dust, smooth fabrics keep clean for longer and dark fabrics *look* clean for longer.

9. Add *the decorative edging*. This can be stuck down with Copydex, or tacked with decorative gold-headed tacks.

10. The last stage is to tack *a hessian backing* underneath the chair to tidy it up and keep out the dirt.

Re-upholstering Unsprung Chairs
The best examples of unsprung chairs are dining-room chairs with drop-in seats.

1. Take the upholstery apart, using the opportunity to mend and clean the woodwork.

2. Following the method already described, tack *new webbing* to the drop-in frame, but attach it to the *top* of the frame, not the underneath.

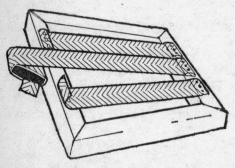

3. Cover the webbing with a layer of *hessian*, tacked down to the frame. This will take the padding.

4. As before, tack loops to the hessian to anchor *the stuffing*. Clean and air the old padding, or buy new if you prefer, and tease it through the loops. Concentrate the padding in the centre but make sure the wooden frame is amply covered, or it will be a very uncomfortable seat.

5. Cover the padding with *calico*, tacked down at the edges.

6. Cover this with *a decorative cover*, using the original worn cover as a pattern.

7. Tack *a hessian cover* under the frame to keep out dirt.

Padding Boxes and Trunks

Cover the top of the box or trunk with a thick layer of kapok or foam cut to size; then add a decorative cover. The box can be lined with material which is either stuck in or tacked in; you can pad it lightly with wadding if you wish. This is a particularly good idea if you are going to adapt small boxes as jewellery cases, or larger boxes or piano stools as work boxes.

Useful Books

Books

Burdett, Eric, *The Craft of Book Binding*, David & Charles, 1975.

Bradford, Ernle, *Teach Yourself Dictionary of Antiques*, The English Universities Press Ltd, London, 1963.

Cross, Rena, *China Repairs and Restoration*, Drake Publications, 1973.

Doussy, Michel, *Antiques: Professional Secrets for the Amateur*, Souvenir Press, 1973.

Hart, Dorothy M. and Halliday, John, *Simple Upholstery*, Dryad Press, 1968.

Innes, Jocasta, *The Pauper's Homemaking Book*, Penguin Books, 1976.

Kelly, Francis, *Art Restoration*, David & Charles, 1973.

Kinney, Ralph, *The Complete Book of Furniture Repair and Refinishing*, Charles Scribner's Sons, New York, 1971.

Plenderleith, H. J. and Werner, A. E. A., *Conservation of Antiques and Works of Art: Treatment, Repair and Restoration*, Oxford University Press, London, 1972.

Pond, Thomas, *Mending and Restoring China*, Garnstone Press, London, 1970.

The Collector's Series, Country Life, London.

Richardson, Nellie and Morton, Will, *Mending and Restoring Upholstery and Soft Furnishings*, Garnstone Press, 1973.

Savage, George, *The Art and Antique Restorer's Handbook*, Barrie & Jenkins, 1968.

Wells, Susan, *Mend Your Own China and Glass*, G. Bell and Sons Ltd, 1975.

Pocket Books

Banister, Judith, *English Silver Hallmarks*, W. Foulsham & Co. Ltd, Slough, 1970.

Fisher, Stanley William, *English Pottery and Porcelain Marks*, W. Foulsham & Co. Ltd, Slough, 1970.

Jackson, Radway, *English Pewter Touchmarks*, W. Foulsham & Co. Ltd, Slough, 1970.

Periodical

Art and Antiques Weekly, Morland Publications Ltd, 2 Arundel Street, London, WC2.

Proper Precautions

Some of the products mentioned in this book are toxic or highly inflammable, and many of the tools are potentially dangerous. Be sure to read and follow the manufacturer's instructions. Protect your hands with rubber gloves if you're using products like caustic soda and paint stripper, and if you get any on your skin, wash it off at once. If you're using something like ammonia, which has powerful fumes, work out of doors if at all possible – and if that's out of the question, work by an open window and air the room thoroughly. When using a substance which catches fire swiftly and fiercely – petrol, for instance – don't smoke while you're working or splash it around near the gas stove. Keep tools and equipment in a locked cupboard, high up out of a child's reach, and make sure that any poisonous, toxic or inflammable (or 'flammable') products are locked safely away. Have a properly equipped First Aid box to hand, so that you can deal with cuts, grazes, and so on. Note down the doctor's phone number, and just to be absolutely sure, check on the whereabouts of the nearest Casualty Department in case a child manages to overcome all these precautions.

The Royal Society for the Prevention of Accidents say that the following proprietary products, Araldite, Benzene, Benzole, Chloramine T, Dabitoff, Domestos, Durofix, Polystrippa, Thawpit and Treasure Wax or Liquid Leaf, should all be stored and used with care, according to the manufacturer's instructions, since some toxic or inflammable hazard exists; the manufacturer's instructions should be followed with *all other* proprietary brands. Check with the maker if in any doubt. Among the other substances mentioned, similar hazards are known to exist with acetone, pure alcohol, ammonia, aniline dye, borax, carbon disulphide, carbon tetrachloride, caustic soda, hydrogen peroxide, kerosene, methylated spirit, and surgical spirit. And a possible hazard is known to exist with fibre glass, french polish, fuller's earth, glass/sand paper, linseed oil, oil of eucalyptus, steel wool, turpentine, washing soda and white spirit. About a number of the other commodities the Society couldn't comment for certain – but they did give seven an absolutely clean bill of health. These were beeswax, bran, glycerine, gold leaf, paraffin wax, titanium dioxide – and distilled water! All recognised as inert and non-toxic.

So take the proper precautions.

Index

hesive, 18; when protecting pictures against dirt, 64

hallmarks: on gold, 32; on silver, 34
hammers: cabriole, 11, 105; rubber, 36
handles: china, modelling replacements for, 20; furniture, replacing, 73–4, 85–6
hatstands, 74
hessian, in upholstery, 107, 112
hinges, 41; mending, 41; replacing, 85–6
horsehair, in upholstery, 107
humidifiers, electric, 72
hydrogen peroxide, as bleach, 15, 51, 55, 104, 116

ink stains, removal from fabrics, 103–4
Insectrol, insecticide, 61
iron, 40; cleaning, 40; restoring, 40–41
iron mould, on fabrics, 104
ironing: removal of grease by, 48–9, 55, 104; smoothing prints by, 51–2

jet, cleaning and repairing, 45
jeweller's rouge, for removing scratches, 23, 33, 34
jewellery, 30; cleaning, 34–5
Joy french polish, 96; and scratch dressing, 87

kapok, in upholstery, 107
kerosene, as antidote for acetone in removing varnish, 54, 116
knot holes, knotting for concealing, 95

lace, cleaning of, 101
lacquers: for copper and brass, 39; for papier mâché, 62; scented, 74; spray, 98; for wood, 99
lamps: conversion of bottles, etc., to, 27–9; oil, 42
latex foam, in upholstery, 107
leather book-bindings, 46, 47; cleaning, 57; mending, 58–9; restoration of gilding on, 60
lemon juice: for cleaning copper and brass, 38; with salt, for removing stains from fabrics, 103
linseed oil, treating wood with, 93, 116–17; liquid gold, 60, 99; see also Treasure
locks, 41

magnesia powder, for cleaning furs, 102
mahogany, 73
marks, maker's, on china, 13; see also hallmarks
marquetry, 87
masking tape: when cleaning metal fittings, 39; when mending metal, 37
metal brackets and plates, for strengthening repairs. 66, 71, 83–4
metal polishes, 23, 33, 34–6, 38
metallic paints and waxes, 37, 38, 98, 99
metals, 31; see also brass, copper, gold, iron, silver
methylated spirit: for cleaning velvet, 102; as solvent of glue, 17, 80; and grease, 15, 17, 65, 86; stain remover for fabrics, 102; precautions with, 116

Prices and postage and packing rates shown below were correct at the time of going to press.

FICTION

All prices shown are exclusive of postage and packing

General Fiction

☐ THE CAIN CONSPIRACY	J. M. Simmel	£1.20
☐ HMS BOUNTY	John Maxwell	£1.00
☐ A REAL KILLING	William Keegan	80p
☐ SEARCHING FOR CALEB	Anne Tyler	95p
☐ CELESTIAL NAVIGATION	Anne Tyler	95p
☐ THE ENTREPRENEUR	I. G. Broat	£1.00
☐ THE SOUNDS OF SILENCE	Judith Richards	£1.00
☐ THE BOTTOM LINE	Fletcher Knebel	£1.25
☐ ON THE BRINK	Benjamin Stein with Herbert Stein	95p
☐ CHAINS	Justin Adams	£1.20
☐ SUPER TOUR	Marilyn Allen	95p
☐ RUNNING SCARED	Gregory McDonald	85p
☐ DISCOTHEQUE	Steven Gaines	85p
☐ THE TUCSON CONSPIRACY (Western)	Matt Chisholm	75p
☐ THE INDIAN INCIDENT (Western)	Matt Chisholm	75p

Crime Thriller

☐ THE TWO FACES OF JANUARY	Patricia Highsmith	95p
☐ A GAME FOR THE LIVING	Patricia Highsmith	95p
☐ THE BLUNDERER	Patricia Highsmith	95p
☐ THE TREMOR OF FORGERY	Patricia Highsmith	80p
☐ SNOWBIRD	Larry Levine	85p
☐ STRAIGHT	Steve Knickmeyer	80p
☐ FIVE PIECES OF JADE	John Ball	85p
☐ IN THE HEAT OF THE NIGHT	John Ball	85p
☐ THE EYES OF BUDDHA	John Ball	85p
☐ GAMES	Bill Pronzini	85p
☐ THE INSANITY MACHINE	Peter Maxwell	85p
☐ THE HANGED MEN	David Harper	80p
☐ THE PEKING PAY-OFF	Ian Stewart	90p
☐ THE TEN-TOLA BARS	Burton Wohl	90p

Romance

☐ NIGHTINGALE PARK	Moira Lord	90p
☐ ROYAL FLUSH	Margaret Irwin	£1.20
☐ THE BRIDE	Margaret Irwin	£1.20
☐ DAUGHTER OF DESTINY	Stephanie Blake	£1.25
☐ FLOWERS OF FIRE	Stephanie Blake	£1.00
☐ THE WHISPERING ROCKS	Sandra Heath	80p
☐ LOVE'S SCARLET BANNER	Fiona Harrowe	£1.20
☐ MYSTIC ROSE	Patricia Gallagher	£1.20
☐ CAPTIVE BRIDE	Johanna Lindsey	£1.00

Science Fiction

- [ ] THE OTHER LOG OF PHILEAS FOGG   Philip Jose Farmer   80p
- [ ] THE LION GAME   James H. Schmitz   70p
- [ ] THE WITLING   Vernor Vinge   75p
- [ ] GRIMM'S WORLD   Vernor Vinge   75p
- [ ] A TOUCH OF STRANGE   Theodore Sturgeon   85p
- [ ] THE SILENT INVADERS   Robert Silverberg   80p
- [ ] THE SEED OF EARTH   Robert Silverberg   80p
- [ ] BEYOND THE BARRIER   Damon Knight   80p
- [ ] THE FLORIANS   Brian M. Stableford   80p
- [ ] FURY   Henry Kuttner   80p
- [ ] THE MAKESHIFT ROCKET   Poul Anderson   70p

Horror Occult

- [ ] POE MUST DIE   Marc Olden   £1.00
- [ ] ISOBEL   Jane Parkhurst   £1.00
- [ ] THE HOWLING   Gary Brandner   85p
- [ ] SPIDERS   Richard Lewis   80p

Film TV tie in

- [ ] TYCOON   Scott Marshall   90p
- [ ] GENERAL HOSPITAL: THE SHADOWED HEART   Max Marquis   75p
- [ ] WUTHERING HEIGHTS   Emily Brontë   80p
- [ ] DRIVER   Clyde B. Phillips   80p

NON-FICTION

☐ KILLING TIME	Sandy Fawkes	90p
☐ ITV'S GREENHOUSE GARDENING	Keith Fordyce and Claire Rayner	75p
☐ JAMES HUNT AGAINST ALL ODDS		80p
☐ LEARN BRIDGE WITH REESE	Terence Reese	85p
☐ THE HAMLYN BOOK OF CROSSWORDS 1		60p
☐ THE HAMLYN BOOK OF CROSSWORDS 2		60p
☐ THE HAMLYN FAMILY GAMES BOOK	Gyles Brandreth	75p
☐ THE HAMLYN CARTOON COLLECTION		70p
☐ STAR-FILE ANNUAL (Ref)	Dafydd Rees	£1.50
☐ THE OSCAR MOVIES FROM A–Z (Ref)	Roy Pickard	£1.25
☐ THE HAMLYN FAMILY MEDICAL DICTIONARY (Ref)		£2.50
☐ BLACK SATURDAY (War)	Alexander McKee	80p
☐ LONELY WARRIOR (War)	Victor Houart	85p
☐ BLACK ANGELS (War)	Rupert Butler	£1.00

Kitchen Library

☐ THE BEST OF DIAL-A-RECIPE	Audrey Ellis	80p
☐ MIXER AND BLENDER COOKBOOK	Myra Street	80p
☐ PASTA COOKBOOK	Myra Street	75p
☐ HOME BAKED BREADS AND CAKES	Mary Norwak	75p
☐ MARGUERITE PATTEN'S FAMILY COOKBOOK		95p
☐ EASY ICING	Marguerite Patten	85p
☐ HOME MADE COUNTRY WINES		40p
☐ COMPREHENSIVE GUIDE TO DEEP FREEZING		40p

All these books are available at your local bookshop or newsagent, or can be ordered direct from the publisher. Just tick the titles you want and fill in the form below.

NAME ....

ADDRESS..

....

Write to Hamlyn Paperbacks Cash Sales, PO Box 11, Falmouth, Cornwall TR10 9EN
Please enclose remittance to the value of the cover price plus:
UK: 22p for the first book plus 10p per copy for each additional book ordered to a maximum charge of 92p.
BFPO and Eire: 22p for the first book plus 10p per copy for the next 6 books, thereafter 4p per book.
OVERSEAS: 30p for the first book and 10p for each additional book.

Whilst every effort is made to keep prices low it is sometimes necessary to increase cover prices and also postage and packing rates at short notice. Hamlyn Paperbacks reserve the right to show new retail prices on covers which may differ from those previously advertised in the text or elsewhere.